Listen to the Mountains

Listen to the Mountains

A Himalayan Journal

PAMELA CHATTERJEE

Illustrations by
CATHERINE ADDOR-CONFINO

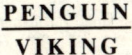
PENGUIN
VIKING

VIKING

Published by the Penguin Group

Penguin Books India Pvt Ltd, 11 Community Centre, Panchsheel Park,
New Delhi 110 017, India

Penguin Group (USA) Inc., 375 Hudson Street, New York, New York 10014, USA

Penguin Group (Canada), 90 Eglinton Avenue East, Suite 700, Toronto,
Ontario, M4P 2Y3, Canada (a division of Pearson Penguin Canada Inc.)

Penguin Books Ltd, 80 Strand, London WC2R 0RL, England

Penguin Ireland, 25 St Stephen's Green, Dublin 2, Ireland
(a division of Penguin Books Ltd)

Penguin Group (Australia), 250 Camberwell Road, Camberwell,
Victoria 3124, Australia (a division of Pearson Australia Group Pty Ltd)

Penguin Group (NZ), cnr Airborne and Rosedale Roads, Albany,
Auckland 1310, New Zealand (a division of Pearson New Zealand Ltd)

Penguin Group (South Africa) (Pty) Ltd, 24 Sturdee Avenue, Rosebank,
Johannesburg 2196, South Africa

Penguin Books Ltd, Registered Offices: 80 Strand, London WC2R 0RL, England

First published in Viking by Penguin Books India 2005

Copyright © Pamela Chatterjee 2005
Illustrations copyright © Catherine Addor-Confino 2005

All rights reserved

10 9 8 7 6 5 4 3 2 1

Typeset in *Sabon Roman* by SÜRYA, New Delhi
Printed at Sanat Printers, Kundli, Haryana

For Pratap,
whose cherished values remain . . .
and Kaveri, Anjali, Aliya, Ilina and Tara,
who have his treasured inheritance . . .
. . . and also, the other granddaughters of the
Himalayas, from whom I learn to listen to the
mountains.

Contents

Acknowl... ...ments

M
...y thar...
...treasu...
Ravi B... ...
Simoes and ...
My fam...
concern is v...
Ella, who ha...
and Dubby ...
words and ...
Sarla an...
since my cha...
Mirai-B...
me.
Cathery...
with the debt...

Acknowledgements

My thanks for advice on the manuscript and reassurance to a first-time author to:

Ravi Dayal, Anita Desai, Ayesha Kagal, Frank Simoes and Ravi Singh.

My family and close friends whose support and concern is valued—in particular to Ashoke and Romir-Ella, who have been right there for nearly fifty years, and Dubby who has an inimitable flair for the right words and many other things.

Sarla and Indi with whom I have shared so much since my childhood.

Mirai-Binoy and Pria-Jay, who are always there for me.

Catherine Addor-Confino, for the illustrations done with the dedication she gives to every task.

Author's Note

The names of people in the various incidents mentioned have been changed; also, for better readability, adjustments have been made in the sequence of events and happenings. All the incidents are from Uttaranchal except three or four from Uttar Pradesh.

The common names of birds are taken from Salim Ali's *Indian Hill Birds*.

Introduction

In my childhood days—a very long time ago—the Himalayas loomed large in my life. I spent hours speculating on an enchanted ride on the clouds to the snow-clad peaks. But all these years later, more than the sight of the mountains themselves, I remember fragments of life in the mountains, like being awakened in the morning by the song of the whistling thrush, the chattering of the white-cheeked bulbul, or the merry call of the crested black tit. Other memories come rushing back: the red-billed blue magpie with its long tail spread out, gliding by the balcony; voices of my friends from the village, as they clamber up the hill to deliver milk; purple-smudged hands gathering berries from the *kilmora* bushes; soft-furred calves frolicking near their mothers who graze contentedly; the aroma of freshly dug potatoes being cooked on a charcoal fire; the hypnotic rhythm of drums at the *jagar* ceremonies . . .

These memories affected my thinking and approach to life even after I moved away to the big cities of the plains. Having lived among people shaped and moulded by the Himalayas, I was always drawn by their understanding of the oneness of nature and man that enabled them to live in harmony with their environment.

Later, I was to spend over thirty years in Mumbai. The city gave me much. The ocean gave me a perspective on my life, which had its own little eddies and storms, its quiet and joyous moments. In Mumbai I saw my two daughters grow up into women with opportunities to build their own lives. There were close relationships with family and other remarkable people. It was a bustling, busy life full of stimulating activities.

Yet, whenever I visited the Himalayas, there was an indefinable joy, and also a longing, which I could not explain to the ocean that had nurtured me all these years in its own generous way. I could not resist the magical pull to the landscape of my childhood, and eventually, I decided to return to the mountains, to make my home in a small village in Kumaon. To live with the trials and comforts of spring, monsoon and winter, which have a distinct character in the Himalayas. And to be with the people who, shaped by an arduous existence, have a tranquillity that reflects a remarkable confidence to meet life's challenges.

It is now thirteen years since I came back to the Himalayas. I have, in some ways, identified with the way of life here. This has brought me the awareness that, ultimately, everything is linked; nothing and no one suffers or flourishes alone. This journal is a record of this connection.

SPRING

The apricot trees are covered with lace-like flowers again, and last night's rain has flecked the buds on the peach trees with pearls. The bulbuls flitting in the branches shower the pearls on the flowers that cover the hillside.

Spring arrives capering and frolicking through the fields, alive with green shoots of wheat and mustard plants. She tugs and pulls mischievously at the misty haze, revealing the mountains, which emerge, benign, constant, unperturbed by her pranks.

* * *

The snow has cleared from the lower mountains. Winter has ended. The buds can no longer keep their tightly held secret and blaze as scarlet roses in a joyous welcome to spring. Among them all, there is one with a delicate blush, which, unruffled, still holds its mystery. Like someone glimpsed briefly in a crowd, a stranger whom I never saw again, but whose memory, stirring and vivid, has stayed with me.

* * *

Then the snow melts on the ground and the bare, soggy soil is soon transformed into a green carpet. Not to be outdone, the trees adorn their bare branches with glistening green and pink buds. And almost overnight there is a burst of colour on the hillside, with flowers craning perkily from every chink and crevice—just to bloom, briefly, in splendour.

I stopped to rest awhile, preoccupied with my concerns. But the frolicsome breeze danced over me, till I woke up to the message of spring. I felt revitalized, for the aches and pains of the cold winter would soon fall away.

*   *   *

It is mid-March, the first day of the month of *Chait*, which is the New Year in the Hindu calender. It is celebrated with *Phul-Dehali*—the giving of flowers. Unheeding of the call of their parents, the children run off, climbing trees to collect the gorgeous rhododendron flowers or scrambling on the hillside for wild daisies and lilies. These are decorated in a thali, along with grains of rice, red-coloured turmeric and yellow sandalwood paste.

The children go from house to house with the thalis, singing and sprinkling flowers and rice on the threshold of each house, so that it is blessed. They are welcomed by people, who apply the sacred paste on their foreheads, put jaggery and coins in the thalis, and also give the children some rice to take home.

The children sprint to the market to buy trinkets

with their coins, while the parents prepare the traditional kheer to give the year an auspicious start.

The delight of the festivity lit up their faces, which made me go along with them. And my self-consciousness was soon forgotten as I got caught in their smiles.

*   *   *

My presence in the village had evoked some interest and curiosity at first: why had I come here? Why all alone? Did I not have a family who could take care of me?

I explained that I had lived in the hills in my childhood and had always wanted to come back to the Himalayas because of the inspiring beauty of these mountains. And that I had two daughters who were married and living in their own homes and I was on my own . . .

'Only two daughters and no husband and not even a son! That is hard on you. But we all have to accept our karma. What else can you do but live alone, as it is not right to live with your sons-in-law. We don't even drink a glass of water in our married daughter's house. Of course you are welcome to stay here and be with us.'

*   *   *

The first wedding of that spring. After all the din and fuss of the wedding was over, Sunita Devi, the young

bride, found herself alone and wept silently for loved and familiar faces. She had been prepared for this right from her childhood, when talk of her marriage was part of the daily conversation. Yet it was too much for her to be wrenched overnight into new surroundings, amongst strangers. It became much worse when the young people in the village surrounded her, unabashedly curious, asking her a volley of questions.

Dewan Joshi, her husband, was kind and sensitive and Parvati Devi, her mother-in-law, was also supportive. But Sunita barely knew them and could not really turn to them. Seeing her so distraught, Vijay Joshi, her father-in-law, even suggested that he would take her to spend some time with her family.

But in a few days, there is a glow on Sunita's face. She runs to fetch her father-in-law's hookah, goes cheerfully with her mother-in-law to gather fuelwood and washes her husband's clothes while he hums and sings happily.

I too had changed homes, cities. Each time it had been hard to move to the unknown and unfamiliar. But so much that has enriched my life was made possible with each change.

*   *   *

The hillside is aflame with scarlet flowers of the rhododendron trees. As we climb higher, the tree is smaller and the flower a softer red. Higher up still, at the base of the snowline, the rhododendron is no longer a tree, but an unfamiliar, scraggy bush with elfin flowers, pink, yellow and white.

At each stage the flower has its own radiance, which is in harmony with the beauty of the surroundings.

It was seemingly difficult to develop an affinity with people whose ways and habits were different, until I discovered in them the same human qualities that we all value and cherish.

*   *   *

Kalavati Devi was widowed young and had only one daughter, Hema. Her brother Puran Negi had given her a small piece of land from his own little plot, just enough to build a one-room house, with the help of a scheme for poor women in her position. She managed to eke out a living by working in neighbours' fields and doing odd jobs. Hema was the joy in Kalavati's life and the mere thought of her made her smile. Her happiness knew no bounds when Puran arranged a match for Hema and provided a few clothes and a thin gold ring each for the young couple, as well as one for the presiding priest.

It was a difficult prospect for her to live alone, without Hema, but she always cheered herself with the thought that her daughter now had a home of her own. Also, she could look forward to her visit, once a year. In time, there was a little granddaughter for whom Kalavati would send a few cobs of corn and cucumbers from the little patch in front of her house.

Kalavati was shattered when Hema's young husband was taken ill with an undiagnosed stomach pain. Despite the efforts of the local doctor, he could not be saved. His parents told Hema that she had brought bad luck to the family and, there being no grandson, they really had no use for her. She was sent back to her mother along with her little girl and told never to step into their village again.

Kalavati and her daughter began to live together, as they had lived before, but now they had the little girl to make them both smile.

Sometimes we are swept away unexpectedly by dark

forces beyond our control. But just as inexplicably, they seem to wilt and let go of their hold.

*   *   *

Today is Basant Panchami, the festival which marks the advent of spring. The rich smell of sizzling puris and halwa tells us that there is to be a feast. The children call out to each other to bring out shirts, pyjamas, saris or even handkerchiefs to be dyed bright yellow. Friends and relatives arrive in yellow clothes and enjoy each other's sweets and talk animatedly about seeds and the sowing of crops. In the midst of the bustle and activity no one seems to notice that it is rather cold for spring and plantings may even have to be delayed.

After a point, the real purpose of the festival did not matter. It had become a tradition that they valued.

*   *   *

Dewan Joshi has come home on leave from his army posting, after an absence of almost a year. People in the village surround him and children bow and touch his feet, and he digs into his pocket to bring out sweets for them. He barely exchanges a word with Sunita Devi, his wife, who looks at him shyly when he hands his bags to her. But there is a sparkle in her eyes as she bustles around with new-found energy to make tea for everybody. She, who was withdrawn and quiet while he was away, is able to give of herself again.

The letters I await from my daughter are intermittent and matter-of-fact. Then, unexpectedly, she arrives, and her smile expresses all the caring I could wish for. And I realize that that is her way of love.

*   *   *

People in the inaccessible mountain village are dependent on each other and have a strong sense of mutual respect. But Bishan Kathayat had been away in the big city for many years and on his return set about aggressively establishing himself. He pushed himself forward at village meetings, at temple prayers and whenever officials came to distribute fruit saplings or medicines.

Everyone was intimidated by his imagined powers and mutely watched him. Meanwhile, Bishan became bolder and even inched his way into his neighbour's fields. This was too much for Vijay Joshi, who, together with his son Dewan, confronted Bishan. Soon enough, the rest of the village came out solidly behind them.

Bishan muttered to himself about the changes in the village which no longer had respect for a well-established city-returned person like him, and he remained aloof with his family. But, in time, the isolation irked him and slowly he was drawn back into the life he had known and the camaraderie of old friends.

Like most people in this village and elsewhere, I too am moved by the injustice of a distressing situation, but continue to live with it, waiting absurdly for someone else to take the lead, hoping things will resolve themselves.

*   *   *

The imposing old oak stands by itself on the slope above the terraced fields. The tiny acorn from which it germinated decades ago could have come there in many ways: carried by the wind from the nearby forest, carried by birds winging their way through the trees, shed by animals browsing there, or perhaps planted by someone.

The seed survived the winter snow and the summer drought, and escaped the grazing goats and cows. It sprouted and grew into a sturdy bush, and, over the years, emerged as this splendid tree.

The ideas I live by stem from many sources: my intuitive self; the people around me; knowledge gained from books; or sheer chance. Over the years, these ideas have taken deep root and impel me to live the way I do.

*   *   *

Gradually, over the months, I discovered the underlying tensions in the village: the caste groupings of Pandits,

Thakurs and Harijans, the problems between neighbours over the use of water, the disagreements between brothers over the division of land and the resignation of daughters-in-law to endless work. And sometimes these tensions boiled over into bitter quarrels.

But when I visited Vijay Joshi, people gathered around in his courtyard, welcoming me in their shy way. There was a flurry of activity in the kitchen as Sunita Devi boiled water with tea leaves, ginger and freshly ground pepper. The milk came from Bishan Kathayat's house and Tara Dutt provided the sugar. And though Mohan Ram, as a Harijan, was not involved in the kitchen, he was persuaded to sing a song from the *Ramayana*—which he usually sang at jagar ceremonies. It was nice to see this friendly atmosphere, despite the ill-feeling that surfaced occasionally.

As for me, even minor discords with people still affect my composure. I have to make an effort just to be civil.

*   *   *

Whenever Dewan Joshi comes home on leave, he and Mohan Ram meet often in the evenings to smoke a hookah with their neighbours. When the hookah is passed around, Mohan, who is the only Harijan in the group, quietly detaches the wooden section of the pipe and smokes directly from the clay cup that carries the tobacco. No one seems to notice and they all talk and laugh as old friends. Sometimes they decide to stay on and eat the evening meal with Dewan. Sunita Devi serves all of them, but while the others eat in the kitchen, Mohan eats near the door and continues to chat with them.

Dewan agrees that times have changed, and they do have tea together at the local tea shop. But the memory of Mohan's grandfather, Hansram, collecting the carrion from all the houses still lingers and it is difficult to erase all differences when at home; also, to do so would not go down well with the community.

One day when Sunita had her monthly period, Mohan happened to come to the house. He sat outside waiting for Dewan but he did not have his usual cup of tea. For this was the one time, he, an untouchable, would not accept tea from Sunita, who was 'unclean'.

Though all was well on the surface, the difference in treatment did hurt. And when the opportunity came, Mohan made his point, if only to soothe his bruised pride.

*   *   *

Everyone in the village gets to know when any woman there has her monthly 'unclean period', for then she has to be careful not to touch anyone, not even her children. She has to eat separately, sleep in the corner room alone, or even in the cattle-shed on a heap of straw to save on bedding having to be thoroughly washed after the event. At this time she cannot cook or do any of the chores inside the house. The family has to somehow manage while she remains an outcast for about four days.

Sunita Devi was distraught because her 'unclean time' would not allow her to take part in the preparations for her brother's wedding. She knew that there could be no quiet compromise, for it could bring bad luck to the family.

But soon enough, Sunita is back to her routine chores. Work begins as soon as she wakes up. Tea has to be made for the household; the buffaloes have to be milked, given water and hay; food has to be cooked for the family; clothes have to be washed and the fields weeded and hoed. If Sunita sits down for a moment, Parvati Devi, her mother-in-law, calls out to her to bring a mat for a visitor, to make tea, or to put the bedding out in the sun.

It is only when she goes to the forest with other young women to collect firewood, fodder leaves, or dry pine needles to keep the cattle warm at night, that the time is her own. To sit for a while, to laugh and talk, to call out to friends across the hill, to eat the spicy lemon chutney made from fresh lemons grown around their homes, or to share a cucumber eaten with garlic salt. The exhausting work of cutting and carrying heavy loads of oak leaves or wood down the steep slopes is worth the price of freedom for a few hours.

* * *

The hills, forested with imposing oak and straight-backed pines, rise above the terraced fields and clustered villages. And range upon range extends into the horizon, with the green of the forests giving way to darker hues. In the far distance, the mountains are a purplish blue against the white peaks—Nandaghunti, Trishul, Nanda Devi, Nanda Kot, Panchchuli. The whole panorama harmonizes like a symphony, culling in its vast sweep the ballad and refrain of the many lives it encompasses.

A black eagle swoops down into the valley and up again like an accomplished dancer. It circles above and soars into the sky, steering slowly and moving elegantly with motionless wings, before swooping down again and yet again. It manoeuvres untrammelled, instinctively, in its wide-open domain.

*   *   *

Tara Dutt had spent all his savings on his daughter's wedding. He had bought traditional gold ornaments, utensils and some furniture for the house—all of which would give her a welcome and standing in her new home.

But he ran short of money for the village feast, so he turned to Puran Negi for help. Puran did not even have a spare change of clothes to wear, but he commanded respect, which enabled him to obtain loans for his friend. And when Puran was in need, Tara was always there with whatever he had.

Sometimes it is difficult for me to give what someone wants without first weighing my own needs. Such measured generosity allows a slight shadow to creep into my frank and open relationships.

* * *

While cleaning the rice for the morning meal, Panuli Devi feels the quickening pains within. She realizes that there is not enough time to inform the village midwife and prepares for the event with assurance. But there is trepidation too, because she already has three daughters. Her mother-in-law, Govindi Devi, stands at the door, for if she comes in she would be defiled, and then who would cook the food. Panuli does not utter a sound as the infant slips out into the *paraat*—a large flat basin—which has a little water and some rose petals. She cuts the cord quickly with her husband's shaving blade and proceeds to clean the child.

Govindi retreats disappointed, as she now has a fourth granddaughter. Panuli's husband, Bishan Kathayat, feels let down and goes out with his friend to the market. Panuli smiles reassuringly at her newborn daughter and takes her to Mohini Devi, who has a two-year-old daughter and will suckle the baby for three days, till Panuli's milk is pure and she is allowed to do so herself.

In a few days, when Panuli goes to bring fuelwood from the forest, Govindi takes over the baby, seeing to her needs. Panuli's husband eventually returns home and the child is gradually established as a part of the family.

Their attitude, in many ways, was difficult to accept at first. But in time our association brought new perspectives in my life, as well as in theirs, and narrowed down our differences.

*   *   *

Tara Dutt and his wife Mohini Devi decided to visit the sadhu at the shrine of the blind saint, Surdas, which is a few hours' journey from the village. It was said that the sadhu, blind at birth, was abandoned by his family and brought up by a renowned guru. He had gained immense knowledge and spiritual powers and could see through people and know which pilgrims had come with genuine faith, and which only out of curiosity. For those with faith, his very presence fulfilled their innermost desires.

Tara and Mohini spent the whole day with the sadhu. And when they returned with renewed hope and confidence, people knew that the sadhu had been able to help them. And they, too, resolved to go the following year.

Their spiritual beliefs seemed to inspire them with a humane understanding of life. Perhaps my own search to find an intellectual basis for my faith should be preceded by a more receptive mind.

*   *   *

Mohini Devi teaches in the primary school in the village. She walks fast down the hill and up again to the ridge and is there to ring the bell right on time. Children scramble from different directions, chattering and calling out to each other. There is a brief silence for the morning prayers before the clamour begins again.

The bell rings a second time and the children lay out strips of jute on which they sit down to study. Mohini looks sternly at anyone who dares to make a noise or disturb the class—even Munni, her small daughter who cannot be left alone at home, is disciplined. At times Mohini waves a stick at the especially boisterous ones. Subdued and quiet, the children sit for hours writing in their notebooks, reading aloud and chanting their arithmetic tables.

At long last, the bell rings yet again and the children are let loose for the break. They chase each other down the hill and run to the stream below to splash and wade. They climb the chestnut tree and challenge each other to reach the highest point. The sullen, apathetic children in the dull classes are transformed with the liberty to be themselves again.

Watching them, I am reminded of my own daughters, who were most alive and energetic whenever

I brought them to the mountains, where travel is as much a delight as the joy of arriving. The tiny paths led us past small hamlets where we stop for a glass of tea and listen to the village news and also tell them ours. We go past ripening fields of wheat flecked with mustard stalks, pocket-sized plots of dwarf coriander plants with small purple flowers and scattered patches bristling with straight shoots of onion and garlic.

After we climb the ridge and enter the forest, a soothing breeze brings with it the fragrance of pine trees and wild flowers. As we approach our journey's end, the children of the village rush out and announce our arrival. We are ushered in with warmth and laughter and sit around the kitchen hearth to drink piping hot tea, laced with ginger and pepper.

The natural, unadorned pleasures of life touched a chord within, which was forgotten in the tumult of our exacting lives in the city.

*   *   *

Sunita Devi, who had never been away from the hills, was going to the city. She was accompanying Parvati Devi, her mother-in-law, who wanted to visit her younger son, Ranajit Kathayat, working in a factory there. It was a well-deserved respite for Sunita, who had recently been ill but still had to do many of the household and field chores.

Ranajit's family welcomed her and took time off to take her around the city. But after a few days Sunita

started pining for her home, her cows and buffaloes, the smell of crops in the fields, the feel of wet earth, the song of the whistling thrush and the call of the turtle dove, and the company of other women in the village. The backbreaking work of weeding and hoeing in the fields and the endless chores receded into the background. She remembered only the happiness of living in a world that was hers.

I was moved to give a break in life to the little girl who hung about aimlessly in the neighbourhood, and took her in to live with us. But after a few days she scrambled back to those she loved, in the crowded hut which was home.

*   *   *

In the crack between two rocks, where there is a little soil and some moisture, a seed has taken root, but through the long, cold winter there is no sign of life. In spring, tiny green sprigs appear, which in a few weeks grow into tall prickly stalks and find their way to the light, each holding up a delicate blue poppy.

In these mountains, our struggle for survival on the perilous slopes brings out stirring qualities in the young people, revealing an inner strength that we do not recognize in less trying times.

*   *   *

I had brought along some storybooks for children and a few medicines for minor ailments. In a few days children started to come for the books and women for medicines to cure headaches, body aches, coughs and colds. And gradually I became familiar with the women and children in the village.

Panuli Devi came now and again for medicines for her backaches, which were due to carrying heavy loads of wood. When I heard that Bhavna, her infant daughter, was ill, I wanted to see her. But I was cautioned to stay away, as Panuli's mother-in-law, Govindi Devi, was treating her grandchild with medicinal herbs and plants and any advice could be construed as thwarting the treatment. However, Bhavna's condition worsened, so much so that the family had no option but to call the medical assistant from the local health centre. He was downcast when he saw Bhavna and said that she was so frail and feeble that at this stage he could do nothing.

I had heard that Bhavna had been suffering from diarrhoea and vomiting and it seemed that her problem was dehydration. Taking my neighbour Mohini Devi with me, we rushed down to Panuli's house. The room was crowded with several relatives and friends who had gathered there to commiserate over the inevitable. Bhavna was wrapped up in blankets and the windows were tightly shut. Panuli was distraught and had not eaten for three days, and as a result her milk had dried up and she could not feed the child.

We opened the windows to let in the fresh mountain air and Mohini helped prepare boiled water with sugar and salt. Bhavna was given the mixture a small teaspoon at a time and, after about an hour she seemed to revive a little. By the end of the day we had managed to get her to drink over a litre of the water—and she had turned the corner.

After this episode there was a lot of discussion in the village, especially amongst women, who had till now believed that when the body was discharging liquids, the only way of stopping it was by not giving any further liquids. Now this new knowledge had come in time to save Bhavna.

*   *   *

The track from the Harijan settlement, where Hansram lives, to the market, meanders down to the stream and up a steep climb. Hansram is old and frail and can no longer work in the fields, but each day he walks the long distance at his own easy pace and gets to the market.

He sits at his friend's shop to feel the activity around him, to hear the goings-on in the villages nearby, to give advice, to sympathize and to bask in the sun with a newspaper. After a few hours he walks back and is content to be with his wife, Manju Devi, children and grandchildren, in his secluded village.

At this age, it is hard to pick up new threads and we

have to make the effort to keep the old fabric from fraying too much.

*   *   *

Puran Negi has only a few small fields and has to supplement his income by working in his neighbours' fields. His wife, Krishna Devi, is busy all day looking after their two sons, collecting fuelwood and fodder, tending the fields and doing other chores in the house. Yet if anyone should happen to pass the house, there is always time enough for her to make a glass of tea, which she serves with small pieces of jaggery, as sugar is comparatively costly. And Puran is always there to lend a hand during celebrations and sad occasions and other activities in the village.

For them, too, vegetables are sent from the

neighbours' fields, and milk when their cow runs dry. People visit them on festivals bearing traditional sweets, and come to see them if anyone in the family is unwell.

In the city, I came home careworn and fatigued after the day's work and there was no room in my life to take on anything else. And like my neighbours', my front door was firmly closed.

*   *   *

The wheat crop, ready for harvesting, is glowing in the bright sunshine, accentuated with flecks of yellow mustard plants. The farmer plants them together, because both crops draw energy from each other and grow better. But he plants paddy on its own, because it needs all the energy from the soil for itself.

Some relationships are a source of mutual strength and growth, but some make such inroads into my life that I feel drained.

*   *   *

Manju Devi was in despair when Hansram, her husband, died. She sobbed that he always came back with sweetmeats for her when he went to the market on his daily walk. And because she enjoyed chewing cloves, he saw to it that there was always a supply at home. And when she returned from the forest, he was there to help her unload the firewood, and then together they drank tea and relaxed by the kitchen fire.

Hansram's brothers thought that they understood her concerns and tried to calm her, saying, 'You and your family will eat what we eat. We will buy your needs like oil, soap and clothes from the market. And we will try to meet all our brother's wishes.'

*   *   *

Parvati Devi's laboured breathing could be heard as she lay in the sun with eyes half closed. Her swollen feet did not seem to belong to her emaciated body. Vijay Joshi had made his wife as comfortable as possible on a cotton mattress below which straw had been scattered to keep out the moisture. The bright pink umbrella brought from the plains by her son Dewan looked incongruous in the surroundings. But it reminded her of him and also kept away the dust from the paddy that her daughter-in-law Sunita Devi was pounding in the courtyard for the afternoon meal.

The people of the village came in turns so that somebody was always with her, pressing and massaging her legs, coaxing her to eat, or just watching over her when she dozed off.

Vijay was very concerned about his wife and wanted to take her to Delhi for treatment. But the prospect of taking her in a palanquin to the road-head, then by taxi to the railway station and onwards in an crowded train compartment was daunting and risky.

So he was in two minds about undertaking the journey. People advised him that as her chances of survival were bleak, and even less if she travelled, at this stage it was better to get medical aid from the local town. That made him decide to keep Parvati at home, amidst her family and the whole village—where she wanted to be.

* * *

Dewan Joshi came home on leave to see his mother. While there, he helped harvest the wheat crop, and later his father decided that Dewan should go across to help Tara Dutt harvest his crop.

Tara and Mohini Devi have a married daughter, and Munni, the younger daughter, is too young to be of much help, so they find it difficult to do all the harvesting work. Vijay had not forgotten that some years ago, when he had hurt his foot badly and could not work in the muddy paddy fields, Tara and his brother Manoj Dutt had come to the rescue and ploughed his fields. This set a tradition for the two families to help each other whenever there was a need.

The compassion and generosity that people had for each other in those arduous conditions were more valuable than anything outsiders like me could give them.

* * *

Saraswati Devi was widowed several years ago and lived with both her sons in distant Rajasthan, where her husband's employers had given her a job. When her mother was ill, her family in the hills did not send the message to her until it was too late; Parvati Devi had already succumbed to her illness. The telegram informing Saraswati about the death was held back by her colleagues. They arranged for her travel and merely told her that her mother was seriously ill. As she boarded the bus, they told her to be brave in the face of any eventuality, which put a nagging doubt in her mind.

When she arrived at the district town, some acquaintances told her that all must be well as a wedding party was expected from her village later in the day. As she walked down from the road-head to the village, the children preoccupied with play replied vaguely to questions about her mother. She dared not ask anyone else and walked with trepidation towards the familiar path home.

Just outside the house, two women who were coming down to fetch water stopped in their tracks when they saw her and started crying. As she stumbled over the threshold, she was surrounded by her father, Vijay Joshi, her brothers Dewan and Ranajit and her nephews and nieces, sobbing and weeping. She saw them in a haze and collapsed, repeating incoherently that she had wanted only to see her mother's face, just one last time.

During my own mother's prolonged illness, I was afraid to leave her alone. But she urged me to go out, saying, 'Even if I die, I have said all I had to say. And now I also need the silence.'

* * *

The time had come for Dewan Joshi to return to his army posting in faraway Assam. Sunita Devi was up early to cook rotis and his favourite spiced potatoes. And then she hoped that she could spend a little time with him, as with all the family around she rarely saw him alone. But she had hardly finished cooking and packing the food for him, when his father, grandmother and siblings, and others from the village, gathered around him.

The thali with red and yellow paste and grains of rice was brought out and tilak applied on Dewan's forehead. He touched the feet of his elders and folded his hands towards the rest, taking in also his wife. That was all.

He walked away slowly, with leaden feet, thinking of his mother, who always gave the final blessing before he left. A young niece followed him with his heavy tin box on her head while his brother Ranajit carried the hand-luggage. Sunita stood with the older people on the edge of the spur, trying to catch a last glimpse of her husband until he was out of sight.

She had waited for the right opportunity to talk to

him. But, before she knew it, he was saying goodbye
and leaving, with so much left unsaid.

*   *   *

Nand Bahadur and Mamta Devi lived in a small room
with their two young children. They had come from
Nepal and worked odd jobs for people in the villages
around. One day there was an unusual flutter and
activity as ten people from Nand Bahadur's village had
turned up unexpectedly. Besides some sweets from
home, they had brought wheat and dal so that Mamta
could cook for everyone. There was much hilarity and
good cheer as they caught up on news.

Mamta and the children, Indra and Pappu, moved
into the small kitchen alcove and all were
accommodated for the night. Early next morning the
contractor who had brought the people from Nepal
arranged for a hut near the worksite. Nand Bahadur
hurriedly borrowed milk, sugar and a large kettle from
neighbours, and his friends were given a warm send-
off with hot glasses of tea laced with pepper.

People in the city were not as accommodating. I had a
friend who told me that her two sons came to visit her
on alternate years during their children's school
holidays. This way the two brothers and their families
hardly saw each other, but she said it would have
crowded her house to have them all come together.

*   *   *

In the hills, there are several alternative ways to go from one village to another: we can follow the stream and then climb slowly up the meandering path, or we can cut across the fields and walk through one or two neighbouring hamlets, or we can take the unfrequented, shorter but more difficult hilly track.

This last is hidden from view by tall trees, bushes and vines. Along the hillside, delicate flowers in pastel colours dot the thick foliage. On the slope below, a large chestnut tree stands out with its candle-like yellow and white flowers. And in the distance we can see the river Gomti as it glistens on its way to the plains. The track winds its way upwards round a sharp bend to a verdant glen encircled by the awe-inspiring peaks. The spell of the scene soothes away the fatigue as we sink into the grass in bliss.

Most roads in the rugged terrain of the region come to an abrupt end and there is only a rough track to remote villages in the interior. Here, people keep to themselves, living for the most part on what they can grow. They venture out once in a while to fairs in small towns, or to visit shrines in the area.

The biggest event in their lives is a wedding in which everyone, irrespective of age, is involved in the preparations and ceremonies. The high point of the activities is when the bride is brought home and the whole village turns out to welcome her. The bright pink canopy on her palanquin can be spotted from afar, with the groom, the son of the house, walking by

her side draped in a red shawl with a multicoloured umbrella held over his head.

The party stops at the road-head and the music gets underway, which must help to distract the bride from the steep slopes which will isolate her from her home. The music is a blend of the traditional Kumaoni and a kind of modern disco, with the blaring of horns and beating of drums mixed with a cacophony of sound from bagpipes and punctuated with loud crackers. It is said that the echoes reach the gods residing in the high mountains, who bless the young couple and all who take part in the event.

*   *   *

Puran Negi had to unexpectedly go to Someswar to meet a relative who was ill. His two sons went to the neighbouring village to visit their uncle just for a day, but were persuaded to stay the night. The impact of the situation did not hit Krishna Devi until she came back from the fields to an empty house. She lit a fire to cheer herself, cleaned the utensils and tidied up the house, but she could not bring herself to cook a meal. She walked to the cowshed to check on the animals and then sat outside looking vacantly into the dusk. She had never been in a house by herself and, indeed, had never slept alone in a room.

Krishna felt that she would choke in the empty space around her, and walked across quickly to her neighbour Panuli Devi and asked if her daughter Chandra could spend the night with her. It was fun to cook the meal with Chandra and they talked and laughed till quite late into the night. Chandra enjoyed the camaraderie of an older woman, and Krishna was relieved to have another person in the house.

*   *   *

Panuli Devi gave birth to her fifth child, and this time the much-wanted son arrived. After four daughters, Bishan Kathayat and Panuli could not contain their jubilation and, moreover, her status with her in-laws went up immediately. Everyone in the village remembers the grand celebration where sweets and saris were distributed generously to announce the infant son's arrival. As he grew up, the boy, who was named Kailash, got the best that they could provide: the only one to get a cup of milk when he woke up; the first to be served food; shoes to wear, while the girls wore rubber chappals; time to play, while the girls were kept occupied with household chores and work in the fields.

The girls were devoted to their brother and seemed to accept the favouritism as a natural fact of life. The unfair treatment meted to the daughters of the house was distressing for me. But Chandra, the thirteen-year-old, said, 'How can we resent him? But for his delayed arrival, we girls would not have been born at all.'

*   *   *

Summer does not usually visit us in the mountains, for spring holds its sway until the monsoon takes over, which in turn bows out when winter spreads its chill. But this year summer has arrived as an unwelcome guest, and the sun beats down harshly through the light mountain air.

The heat has driven away the cooling April showers, leaving the wheat crop dry and shrivelled. Pine needles have turned brown and fallen lifeless to the ground. Tree-sparrows and turtle doves fly around in search of ripened grain, and are shooed away by farmers with the loud beating of drums in an effort to protect their already sparse crop.

There are squabbles over the trickle of water from the mountain streams, as people struggle to save their little patches of tomatoes and chillies. Farmers scan the cloudless sky and begin to worry about feeding their families, for not only is the wheat crop meagre, but also the rice seeds sown in the uplands have not sprouted in six weeks. Women move about restlessly with the unusual lull of inactivity, for weeding and hoeing in the fields is not required. Nature seems to have kept away all intruders from the already struggling crops.

With the dryness all around, the forest is like a tinderbox, and every now and again a fire breaks out, spreading wildly, spewing a dense balloon of smoke. People call to each other and gather to beat out the fire with bushy branches, rushing around with buckets of water from their limited supply. In the face of calamity, they knew they had to work together.

*   *   *

The hailstorm that came late in April lashed the trees mercilessly, knocking down the unripe apricots and plums. The year's labour was lost. Vijay Joshi sat silently, looking at the devastation of his fruit and that of his neighbours, all around. Only the persistent gurgling sound, as he smoked his hookah, revealed his distraught mind.

Slowly, he walked towards his peach trees and reassured himself that the tiny, barely visible buds had survived the storm. Then, as was the norm at times like this, the farmers got together to talk of nature's ways, of the good years and the bad, which in the end evened out—for had they not survived and lived respectably all these years?

There was a time of loss when I felt that destiny had singled me out arbitrarily for such a harsh blow. It is only now that I can see that I had also been given the strength to pull through that bleak period.

*   *   *

The green is slowly turning to gold as the wheat ripens in the spring sunshine. In the warmth of the lowlands,

the wheat crop matures quickly—in about four months. Here, in the hills, it has taken six long months of tending right through the cold winter, and now in late spring the golden grain has ripened.

Over the past six months, women have watched over the crop and tended it with care. At the time of sowing, sagging baskets of manure dwarfing their thin frames were carried to the fields. When there was no rain, they walked with blistered feet through the parched earth to open the channels connected to the mountain stream. And when there was rain, they waded through the churned-up soil to pull out unwanted weeds and shrubs with deft and nimble fingers.

The crop this year has surpassed expectations. The men-folk gathered together on their fields can be seen talking animatedly about the surplus for the market, after the needs of the family have been met. The women and older girls are bustling about excitedly, harvesting and threshing the wheat, while the young boys are filling sacks with the grain.

Over the past two years, the meagre crop was only enough to feed just the village people for half the year; there was no question of any income from the sale of grain. Indeed, many farmers had incurred debts to purchase wheat for their own needs from local merchants.

But in the midst of the present happy time, there is also the awareness that it will be time to plough and sow the field for the next crop . . . and the next, with good or bad harvests to be taken as they come.

* * *

The hamlet located on the north side of the village had no water at all. Women spent up to three hours a day going down to the stream and trudging back, carrying heavy buckets of water up the steep slopes. Things were so bad that it became difficult to find wives for young men living there, as no parents wanted to put their daughters through such hardship. Over the years, several approaches were made to the 'highest quarters' to bring water there, but to no avail.

I persuaded the engineer from the department concerned to come to the village meeting. It was soon clear to him that the water which came down the gradient from the highest point in the town had enough force to push itself up to the hamlet; all it required was a few pipes to convey the water. The prospect of water created a flurry of excitement that caught on even in the neighbouring villages. People enthusiastically helped in the laying of the pipes and, at long last, the little hamlet had water.

It was a moment of pride for everyone who participated, and there was a spontaneous celebration in the hamlet, with tea and sweets for everybody. And for all of us, it was an unforgettable experience of co-operation in the community.

* * *

There was so little land to divide between Bishan and Kundan Kathayat after their father died that somehow each felt that he had been hard done by. The ill-feeling between the brothers came to a head over the use of the water tap. Bishan had bought a drum to store water, but this irked Kundan, who claimed that because of this the limited supply ran out and his family did not get enough.

Their relationship worsened until one day, armed with scythes and sticks, Kundan attacked Bishan's home, and in the melee both were badly injured. The local police arrived on the scene and herded them both into the district jail for the night. But when the children of the two brothers came to visit them and greeted them both with equal respect, it brought home the family bond and the absurdity of their situation.

I went down to the city, where my family had come together to celebrate the hundredth birthday of our aunt. We all wondered what had kept us away from each other for so long, when there was so much to share, and so much affection.

*   *   *

In the mountains, the cloudless, unblemished sky is often aglow with a million stars, which, we are told, revolve and move at incredible speeds. But no matter where we are in the world—in the mountains we know or in distant lands—we see the North Star, the Great Bear, Orion's Belt and others, maintaining their grouping in relation to each other.

Within my own little family, we cannot seem to steer a course which gives us space enough without colliding with one another.

*   *   *

In the silence of the forest, we became aware of the music of the woods: the splash and gurgle of the streams cascading down the hillside; the twitter of the birds interlaced with the toneless chirrup of the cicadas; the droning of the bees amongst the mountain flowers; the grunts of browsing cows mingled with the sound of brass bells; the monosyllabic, low tones of old herdsmen and giggles of young girls collecting firewood.

The din and noise of the city drove me to distraction, till I found its own melody: the mirth and hilarity of the street children; labourers singing companionably of their far-off homes; the animated conversation of the old and retired on their morning stroll; and the lone musician in the market corner, strumming a plaintive tune.

*   *   *

The married women in the village, both young and old, dwell often on the carefree days in their parents' home. No doubt, there, too, they had to work hard, but it was with love and persuasion—not with fear of reprimand. Also, there was fun and laughter as all the siblings shared the work. If they were not well and did not work for a day or two, they were not frowned upon as malingerers, but given care and rest.

Visits by the women to their *maika* or parental home are few and far between, for then 'who would milk the cow, fetch the wood and cut the grass'. But the one time in the year when women could count upon contact with their homes was at *Bhitoli*, during the month of Chait (mid-March to mid-April). At this time it was customary for brothers to visit sisters with gifts of clothes and sweets. The women could not contain their joy on seeing them and eagerly sought news about their parents, family and friends, and questioned them closely about all the little things they missed about their childhood home.

The brothers were required to bring some sweets for each household in the village as recognition of their caring for their sisters. It was a proud moment for the women to be able to distribute something from their homes, no matter that it was just a little jaggery or unclarified sugar on a *timal* leaf. And come Bhitoli, they would scan the road and run out with the sound of a bus, hoping that their brothers had come, at last.

When I moved away from my family in the city to this distant village, I was wistful. I too needed the assurance that all those whom I had grown up with and raised would always be there for me.

*   *   *

Twenty years ago, Bishan Kathayat's marriage was a simple religious ceremony, with the priest blessing the young couple and their families. People from the village brought small gifts: a steel utensil, a copper vessel, or a little cash, and were given tea and some sweets. The women sang ballads which had been a part of weddings for many generations, while the men, dressed in traditional costumes, held swords and shields for the graceful and spirited Kumaoni dance.

But when Bishan returned from his job in the plains, he decided that his daughter Chandra should have a big wedding, in keeping with his status—even at the cost of curtailing day-to-day expenditure. He extended invitations beyond the family circle to the entire village, including the Harijans, for whom there was a special eating area.

In marriages here, every family was given a coconut, as it is an auspicious symbol. The custom spread and as time went on, each one vied with the other to add something to the ritual, giving saris as well to special guests; also, besides the mandatory mangal-sutra necklace, earrings and a nose ring for the bride, there was a bed, a cupboard and other furniture as part of the enhanced dowry.

There is no change in the traditional customs and

religious ceremonies, which continue as of old. The young couples flanked by their parents solemnly seek blessings of the deity, invoked by the chanting of the priest. But now distracting sounds from a 'modern' three-piece band brought from Haldwani intrudes into the solemnity and young lads, looking incongruously like their TV heroes, do a disco dance.

Chandra's wedding ceremony was solemn and traditional, stretching out for almost the whole day. Bishan Kathayat and Panuli Devi, along with other close relatives, sat opposite the groom's family, relishing every moment of this much awaited day. After the formal rituals, there was an exchange of fruit, sweets and gifts, and at this point Chandra had to move to the side of her new family, to whom she would now belong. This was a heart-wrenching moment for her parents, who came forward to embrace her, followed by aunts and uncles, young cousins, nephews and nieces, and all wept unashamedly. Chandra's body trembled imperceptibly with her quiet sobbing.

The video man hired for the occasion waited impatiently to complete his assignment and came forward a few times to remind everyone that the soft light would soon give way to darkness. So Chandra and her new husband, along with several young people, moved to the field where the video scene was directed as in a romantic Indian movie. Chandra, who had only looked at her husband surreptitiously, suddenly found that he had to stroke her hair and look into her eyes and to move around to satisfy the fanciful imagination of the video-man. Fortunately for her, the band struck up and it was time to leave.

Chandra was once again transformed back into the shy, traditional bride, and taken to the deity for a blessing before leaving. She was then guided down the steps of the house, while facing the deity and walking backwards into the courtyard. The family gathered there helped her into the *doli*—the sedan in which she was carried to the road-head. The bagpipes and the dancing and singing of the men from her husband's party drowned the sadness of the final farewell.

When my daughter got married, she decided on a simple ceremony. I would have preferred a more elaborate wedding. But the happiness of the young couple was infectious, and the celebrations and happy clamour that I had desired did not seem relevant anymore.

*   *   *

We wake up to the sharp monosyllabic call of the black-throated jay, and the cheerful, carrying call of the crested black tit. As we listen more intently, there is the characteristic two-tone call of the rusty-cheeked babbler, the musical cadence of the whistling thrush, the melancholy cry of the rufous turtle dove and the repeated, staccato call of the Himalayan cuckoo with the base sounds provided by the loud cawing of ravens.

Dawn responds to this impromptu welcome with a magic dance, changing her costume with deft artistry from a shadowy grey to pink, red and a sparkling crimson. As she bows out, the stage comes alive again with the flapping and rustling of wings. The birds, in their own groupings, take off dramatically or pair off on a romantic journey.

In the city, the dawn came and left unnoticed. The sun streaming through the skylight would awaken me with a start and I would get ready in record speed to dash to work. I knew that the birds had come only because the seeds I had scattered on the balcony were gone.

*   *   *

I always stopped to talk to Kailash and his sister Bhavna whenever I passed their house. But I did not take any notice of Bittu, the nondescript dog they had adopted. He barked and snarled at us and the children had to threaten and scold to quieten him.

One day the neighbour's dog Minoo, with whom Bittu used to play, fell ill. Bittu was noticeably downcast and would sit near Minoo, resting his head on her body. Minoo did not recover from her illness and died. Bittu sat near the spot in the garden where she was buried and moaned loudly for hours and could not be persuaded to eat for several days.

I was touched by Bittu's near-human reaction to the death of his friend. I started talking to him and gave him biscuits whenever I visited Kailash and Bhavna. Now he wags his tail whenever he sees me and follows the children to my house, and sits patiently until I play with him.

I tend to jump to conclusions about people based on their external, superficial behaviour, but when I do reach out to them, I discover warm and interesting facets of their personality.

*   *   *

The farmers planted flowers around their homes, with seeds brought by Dewan Joshi from far-off Assam. Everyone took pride in tending them with care, carrying water for them all the way from the stream at the bottom of the hill. But they were involved the whole day with some activity or the other in the fields or in the neighbouring town, and they had little leisure to enjoy the flowers.

However, nothing could deter Tara Dutt from his passion for his garden. And no matter how late he returned from work, he always spent time with his flowers, taking pleasure in every bloom. This seemed to give them a special glow.

*   *   *

Vijay Joshi was very busy, as he had to go daily to the district town for the court case regarding his land. Normally he spent time with his family and even with his cows, buffalo and bull. But ever since the case began he just rushed off to work, preoccupied with his problems.

One day, as he was walking hurriedly past the house, his tethered bull moved his head forward for attention, but Vijay walked on, immersed in his thoughts. The bull lunged at him and gored his leg, which forced him to stay at home for several weeks.

Sometimes my unthinking comments and actions were hurtful. But it was the occasional neglect and what I left unsaid that provoked a hostile reaction which bewildered me.

*   *   *

Leela Devi had three daughters in succession, in the hope of giving birth to a son. Now she was reconciled to having just daughters and wanted no more children, for she had to work on the farmers' fields to provide for the children she already had. Her husband, Panram, like many other Harijans in the village, was a carpenter, with no land of his own. He worked hard and earned well, but spent most of his money on liquor. Leela dreaded the evenings because, depending on his mood, he would either beat her or demand her love. She had no respect for him but there was no way that she could refuse his needs. She knew, like all the other women, that after marriage she had to do her husband's bidding.

After enduring endless suffering, there came a point when anguish and heartache were like a persistent bodily pain. But she was a spirited person, and no matter how much he bruised and battered her, she would not allow him to crush her spirit.

Leela saved a little money from her meagre earnings, which she kept hidden with a friend. She had hoped that one day this would enable her to leave and go to her parents' home. But her brother, on whom the parents were dependent, made it clear that he would not accept her in the house, especially if she brought along her three daughters. The only relief Leela now had was that she could go for short visits to her mother's sister Manju Devi, who lived in a neighbouring village. Manju was always happy to see her and her daughters and she could find some peace there.

When she missed her monthly period, Leela prayed that it was just an irregularity, but she was worried when the second month went by. She went to the local health centre, but unfortunately the nurse was on leave. Leela could not go unnoticed to the health centre in the nearest town, so she had no choice but to wait. By the time the nurse returned, it was too late to do anything about the pregnancy. Leela was crestfallen, for it was no joy to bear a child forced on her and to feed one more mouth.

But she consoled herself thinking that maybe she

was destined to have a son after all. It could change her husband's attitude, and perhaps her son would grow up and take care of her after her daughters were married.

Leela accepted her fourth pregnancy as a part of her karma. She continued to toil as before, taking care of the household and also working in neighbours' fields. In any case there was no alternative, as her husband was away all day drinking with his friends, in between sporadic jobs. Sometimes Panram stayed away all night and there was no one else at home besides her three daughters and her old father-in-law.

When she was in the eighth month, late one night she felt the familiar pains and knew that her baby was on its way. She woke her seven-year-old daughter, the oldest of the three, to go and call Madhavi, the village *dai*—the midwife. Madhavi was always available for such occasions and was happy to receive a small token gift, unlike the trained nurse at the health centre, who expected some money befitting her status. But Leela's baby was in a hurry and slipped out, whimpering a little, waking her frail, old father-in-law who was sleeping next door. He had kept a new blade for the occasion, which he handed to Leela and withdrew after seeing that, at last, he had a grandson. Leela cut the cord and tied the knot as well as she could by the time Madhavi arrived and took over the child.

Leela got busy clearing up the 'unclean' placenta and afterbirth, which was her own responsibility. She bundled it all in an old newspaper and went to place it under the *bheru* tree. On her return, she smiled when she saw her cleaned and swathed little boy, and proceeded to bathe and clean herself. Madhavi prepared tea for Leela, who, being unclean for ten days, could not enter the kitchen, which would be managed by her aunt Manju, who would come as soon as she got the news. After cleaning the house, Madhavi sprinkled herself with a nettle soaked in cow's urine to purify herself before going home.

Dawn broke in a few hours and Leela went, as usual, to milk the cow and to give it grass and water. As she was not allowed to suckle her baby for the first three days because of her 'impure' milk, Neema, Mohan Ram's wife, who had recently had a baby as well, came to feed the new infant. Leela was a little concerned as the baby seemed to be too weak to suckle and had to be fed drop by drop, but she was distracted by women from the village, who came to congratulate her on the birth of her son.

In the evening the infant barely stirred and did not make a sound, and by nightfall his life ebbed away as quietly as it had come. Leela did not accept his death easily and tried to warm the lifeless body, hugging it closely. The old grandfather gently took the body from her, saying, 'You have three fine children and we cannot expect every bud to bloom.'

Mohan Ram and his great uncle Narayan Ram, who belonged to the extended Harijan family, took the body and buried it near the stream flowing at the edge of the village. Leela lay down in the stillness of the night and wept for her son, whom his father had not even seen.

Although Leela had no heart to do anything, she worked in the house and the fields to the point of exhaustion, so that there would be no time to think of the life that lay ahead.

*   *   *

The little sapling I had planted sprouted a small green bud. And, to my delight, one morning the bud burst open to reveal a wild daisy, which had come unnoticed with the plants from the nursery. The white and gold flower smiled at the world and gave me unexpected pleasure. But the next day the stem was bent low and the flower had a droopy look.

Dismayed, I turned the soil, watered the plant and put it in the sun. The delicate stem responded and stood up again, gently lifting the daisy.

When even a tiny flower can lift my spirits, I need to look more closely at much else that is around me.

*   *   *

Mohan Ram was very busy with his sister Kishori's wedding, for he wanted to make sure that everything went well so that the family's standing would be maintained when the *baraat*—the groom's party—arrived. He got the other young men in the village to help him paint and clean the house and put up coloured streamers for a festive look so that his house would look as good as the Thakur and Pandit homes during a wedding. He told his father to bring kerosene oil for lighting the lamps, as the traditional small earthen wicks normally used would not be appropriate for this occasion. He then went across to the schoolmaster's house to borrow a rug and some chairs for the important guests.

It was a proud moment indeed for the family when the whole village gathered at their house and admired the arrangements. The baraat, though expected in the early evening, arrived at dusk, so everything, including the dinner, had to be delayed. Mohan Ram was unfazed and welcomed the party with brightly lit lamps. Dinner was tastefully served on fresh green banana leaves. But in the middle of the meal, the lamps began to splutter and went off one by one. Mohan Ram was mortified to learn that his father had tried to save a little money by buying only half the quantity of kerosene that he had suggested. He ran desperately to several houses in the village but no one had the luxury of kerosene lamps.

Mohan Ram could not face the idea of the baraat eating in darkness and went and locked himself in the back room. Someone brought out the small earthen wicks whose gentle glow allowed the festivities to continue. But soon after the meal, the light from the wicks, too, began to fade. And there was much humour and jocularity when, after a final drink, the guests were led tripping and stumbling in the darkness to their rooms, so well decorated by Mohan Ram.

The wedding would be remembered for long, though there would be others more elaborate and organized. Like an amateur play that is endearing for its forgotten lines and off-the-cuff delivery.

*   *   *

Everyone said that Vijay Joshi's brother Hyat was blessed by the gods, for after two daughters his wife had two sons. He did everything possible for the children, but every now and again when some clothing or shoes were bought only for the boys, he would say to his wife, 'After all, the girls will belong to another household.' The boys were sent to college in the big town, as there was no college in the small town near their village. But there was no question of sending vulnerable young girls, without their parents, to another town.

As soon as the girls reached puberty, Hyat set about looking for sons-in-law. He wanted to ensure that they were educated and well-employed so that that his daughters would have financial security. He also made discreet enquiries about their character and habits.

Soon after the girls were married, they were

immersed in the activities of a large joint family and could visit their parents only once or twice a year. It was then necessary to find daughters-in-law who would help his wife with all the work. Here, the primary consideration was that they should be capable of hard work and have a reasonably fair complexion. The brides fitted into the household well and everyone felt that fate had indeed been kind to Hyat and he must have done good deeds in a past life.

This ideal state was rudely shaken when, after a year of their marriages, both sons, Jivan and Raghunath, decided to take their wives, Deepa Devi and Janki Devi, to the city with them. Their sons said that, as it was expensive to live in the city, it was not possible for them to provide any financial help to their parents, but they would be welcome in their homes.

Hyat and his wife could not think of leaving their home and their fields, nor indeed their neighbours whom they had known for generations. It would also be hard for them to stay indoors, cooped up in a small room in a crowded city flat on their own all day, while the young people were out to work.

So they decided to manage as best as they could in the village. But in a year or two, the hard work and the heartbreak was evident, as both of them looked worn and old. Their daughters were so distressed that both sons-in-law got together and bought a small flour-grinding maching for Hyat so that he could make a reasonable income while continuing to live in the village. It was hard for Hyat to accept the gift for he remembered that his father would not take anything from his son-in-law's house, not even a drink of water. But everyone convinced him that in his father's days no sons would have dared to take their wives to the city, leaving old parents to fend for themselves. After a while, Hyat had no option but to take the flour-grinding machine, as the income enabled him to pay for manual labour in the fields, which neither he nor his wife could manage at their age.

When the sons visited home, Hyat, and in particular his wife, continued to give them special treatment. But they no longer said that their daughters belonged only to their in-laws' families.

*   *   *

Mohan Ram's niece Ramuli was just an infant when her mother, Kishori, died in an accident when her nylon sari caught fire on the kerosene stove. Mohan Ram, who was devoted to his sister, wanted to keep the baby, but her father would not part with her. His sister, who lived with her in-laws in the neighbouring village, brought up little Ramuli. When she was almost two years old, her father took her over, but as he had to go away on his army postings, she lived for the most part with her old grandfather.

The women of the village felt the sadness of a child without her own mother and took charge of Ramuli. She moved about freely in the neighbouring homes, assuming that they were all her family. She squabbled and played with the children, demanding her share of sweets and bangles and found consolation with their parents in her little troubles. She was loved and welcomed by everyone and seemed to forget the sadness in her life.

Back in the city, I once employed a likeable young man who obviously had had good opportunities in life, and the support of his extended family. But he was temperamental and erratic, and invariably explained his failures by reminding me that destiny had snatched away his father when he was still a child.

*   *   *

In Kumaon, the mountains are considered to be the abode of the gods—'Dev Bhoomi'—and every facet of life is interwoven with the awareness of God. After the birth of a child, spirits are particularly active and the child is allowed out in the sun only after the naming ceremony on the eleventh day. Moreover, the mother too has to be careful and cannot go outside in the sun for at least three days.

Hyat Joshi's daughter-in-law Deepa Devi decided to come back to the village for the birth of her second baby. Her anxious husband Jivan was very involved with his job in the city and felt that the family in the village could take better care of her at this time.

Deepa did not give much importance to the customs in the village and the day after her infant daughter was born, to the horror of the women in the neighbourhood, she went out and slept in the sun. They were not at all surprised when Deepa had a blinding headache and a high fever. They rubbed oil on her head and pressed her limbs, but she became worse and the fever shot up so high that she lost consciousness.

People carried Deepa to the hospital in a palanquin, as the doctor could not be expected to walk down to the village. He confirmed that she was seriously ill and that it would be a risk to keep her in the local hospital. With much difficulty they were able to coax a truck driver to take Deepa, along with some relatives, to the big hospital in Almora.

Deepa lay critically ill for several days. The doctor at the hospital was caring and she was given good medical treatment. But people sought to propitiate the spirits with a ceremony at the hospital conducted by the family priest. Everyone, including the doctors administering the most modern scientific care, subscribed to the belief.

But in spite of all avenues of treatment, Deepa did not survive the illness. Her body was brought back to the road-head of the village and someone called out loudly and persistently right across the hill, announcing the death. People responded by running up the hill towards the truck standing conspicuously on the side of the road.

The body was brought down from the truck on a bamboo stretcher and, as is customary, was placed on the ground. Preparations were then made for the solemn ceremony at the temple, with the women proceeding to break her red glass bangles. Her gold nose ring was removed and six barely discernible slivers shaved off, wrapped in cotton wool and placed on the eyes and the orifices of the ears and nose. This established tradition is based on an ancient belief that this would be payment for the boatman who would safely ferry the soul to that great beyond.

While the men averted their eyes, the women surrounded the bier and removed all clothing and wrapped the body in a white sheet. For all must go unadorned and naked, just as they had come into this world.

The women piled Deepa's clothes in a heap and burned them until there was no trace of anything but the muffled sound of moaning, which wafted in the breeze with the smoke and ash.

The male relatives and other men of the village climbed into the truck as it started up for Deepa's final journey. Her shattered husband, Jivan, clutching his young son Sunder, was inconsolable at the loss of his adored wife.

Then he remembered his newborn daughter and walked quickly towards the house.

A life shared so closely had been lost. But there was the legacy of a new life, which was a ray of hope.

MONSOON

Monsoon clouds take over the sky and even the mighty Himalayas have withdrawn behind the turbulent grey curtain. But in an unexpected calm, the clouds lift slowly to give a glimpse of the breathtaking beauty of Nandaghunti, Trishul and Nanda Devi, each with its own majesty. And even as we look, the clouds descend again and one by one the peaks recede, shrouded in dark, mysterious shapes.

* * *

The gangly datura lily has made an appearance after the first monsoon showers and stands looking down at the array of tiny flowers that have come up on the hillside. The pumpkin seeds planted in early spring have sprouted and grown into a creeper. In between its large fan-like leaves there are bright yellow flowers, and a host of purple-winged butterflies flit amongst them. The bees have heard the news, too, and swarm in for the feast of nectar.

* * *

Vijay Joshi's entire household was up before dawn as it was his turn to transplant paddy in his fields. His son Dewan and daughter-in-law Sunita Devi, after an early bath, sat before the deity in prayer, for a good harvest, while Hira and his cousins swept and cleaned the house.

The children were then given various jobs—to bring down the plough, to yoke the bullocks, to ensure that a constant supply of water was conveyed from the stream, to deliver the paddy saplings from the nursery and to start preparing the food for all those who would be working with them.

During the time of transplating paddy, the fields are flooded and planted in sequence, till everyone's fields are green with saplings. For weeks both men and women have to be out there all day: while the men, splattered in mud, drive the bullocks through the slush to plough the fields, the women stand in ankle-deep water and transplant the seedlings.

The monotony and strain of the backbreaking work is relieved by the singing of the women. Around noon they take a break for lunch. The children of the household in whose fields work is being done bring rotis and piping hot potatoes with chutney. Even though men and women sit in separate groups, there is much teasing and joking as they relax in happy camaraderie.

I am a part of this now, and take it for granted. But in the past I was so involved with my own life that often I lost track of friends. And when I was ready for them, I could not always find a place in their lives.

* * *

The resplendent laburnum tree stood at the corner of the road leading into the village, and people always stopped to chat near it. In summer, its luminous yellow flowers were a landmark for miles around. But this year it fell in the storm which heralded the monsoon. People flocked around in dismay and saw that the trunk, infested by worms, was hollow.

One can maintain a splendid image for the world, I thought, even if one does not live up to that likeness. But not for long.

* * *

Vijay Joshi is up at dawn and calls across the hill to the farmers who have agreed to help harvest his pears. This hard variety of gola pears is suitable for making beer and also jams and jellies, and finds a market in the plains.

Vijay is alert to the drone of a truck as it comes up from the valley, so that he can run to the road to negotiate for transport. While his younger son Ranajit keeps an eye on the work, he walks quickly up to the local market to buy the jute bags for packing the fruit. At the same time, he keeps a wary watch on the temperamental monsoon weather, as a sudden downpour would mean stoppage of work. The whole day goes by in concern and activity until the bags are loaded on trucks and despatched to the plains.

At the end of the day, Vijay relaxes with his family and the farmers who worked with him, drinking steaming hot tea and recounting the day's experiences: of negotiating steep slopes with laden bags; of helpful truck drivers who waited till the bags reached the road-head and the wily one who disappeared after taking money in advance; of the migrant labourer from Nepal who tried to give them the slip with a bag of pears; and of the kindness of Indra, the rain god, who allowed them to work all day.

* * *

The children, too, have their duties. The youngest toddles after the goat with a stick so that it does not stray into the neighbour's field. After school, his sister takes the cows to graze on the hillside, while the elder brother fills in at the shop for his ailing father.

In the evening, they play and run around like children everywhere, and munch roasted corn with their parents around the fire.

* * *

Dewan Joshi had just come back on leave from the army, this time from Ladakh, after seeing action on the Kargil war front. He was surrounded by people who asked him about his work, the dangers he had encountered, the salary he earned, the food he ate, the kind of companions he had and many other questions. His friend Puran Negi basked in Dewan's importance but, after a while, just sat near him silently. Later, when everybody in the market greeted Dewan and offered him tea and snacks, Puran moved away unnoticed.

Dewan and Puran had always done everything together ever since they could remember, and even now they were the best of friends. Puran got left behind because he could not pass the final school-leaving exam, even after his third try. Now he was resigned to his lot, even as a Thakur, to work as a labourer in neighbours' fields, or occasionally on a building site coming up in the nearby town.

His family and other relatives were glad to have him in the village, as most other young people had gone to work in the plains. Puran was obliging and helpful in many ways: he was there to accompany people to the well-known doctor in Gurur when the local doctor could not diagnose a problem; he trudged up to the army canteen with the old pensioners so that they could collect their rum ration; he was able to read letters, manage bank and postal matters and other little things which the village women could not handle on their own. As a result, people all around were kind to him and welcomed him in their homes.

But now it dawned on him that though there was sympathy and affection for him, it was people like Dewan who commanded respect. Puran was now determined to earn people's respect. Everyone missed him and wondered why, after all these years, the quiet, unassuming Puran had suddenly left home to find work in the plains.

*   *   *

The heavy rains washed away the soil from the base of the oak tree, exposing its long thick roots that held up its imposing stature. The oak had always been there, even in the memory of the oldest person in the village, and provided shade in the hot pre-monsoon sun. It required no persuasion to get everybody together to put back the soil to strengthen the base again. But they could do nothing for the tall eucalyptus tree planted only three years ago, which lay on its side awkwardly with its shallow roots torn from the earth.

*   *   *

Bishan Kathayat's mother, Govindi Devi, came to the village as a young bride more than sixty years ago. Now she sits basking in the sun all day and dreams aloud of bygone days: of the children she has raised and those that didn't survive; of the years of flood, drought and bumper harvests; of the hard work in the fields, the laughter and singing in the forests; and the daily load of grass for the cows and buffaloes who provided milk and curds for her children.

She dwells also on the friendship and understanding of women who, like her, came as brides to the village, with whom she still enjoys weddings and festivals. There is, too, the love and respect of the whole village, for whom she is Amma—grandmother.

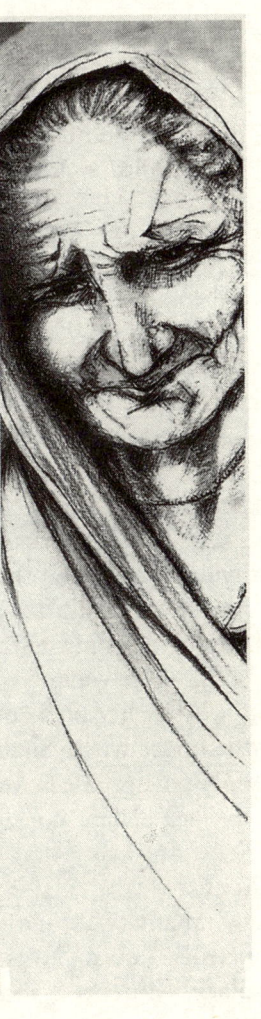

*   *   *

The mahal tree—a wild pear species—had stood in the field for years. All it could do was provide leaves to feed goats in the hot summer months when nothing else was available. The farmer's children were ready to chop down the tree, but he restrained them, saying a new tree in its place would take years to grow.

'You want to change things too quickly by hacking off the root,' the farmer chided the children. 'You'll throw out the valuable with the outmoded.' He decided instead to prune it down and graft a small cutting from a gola pear variety, splicing it and fixing it in position with moist earth.

In spring, new shoots appeared, and in a year, the mahal was taken over by the new pear tree. It bore fruit, which, despite its rock-like hardness, the children munched and enjoyed. Also, it brought a little money as its pulp could be used for jams and chutneys.

*   *   *

When Shanti Devi, who had no children, was widowed, her in-laws did not give her any option but to return to her maternal home. After the death of her parents, her uncle gave her a room to stay in his house, but she had to take care of her own needs. She got a cleaning job in a small shop, which, together with her widow's pension that her uncle had arranged through the district social work department, enabled her to eke out a living. Shanti was cheerful with her lot and felt that life had been kind after all. People admired her spirit and now and again they would give her an old sari or even a shawl in winter.

After her uncle died, his son—her cousin—sold off the house where Shanti lived. She came to know of this only when the new owner came to her room asking her to vacate. Her cousin shrugged his shoulders, saying, 'You are lucky that you have stayed so long without rent.'

Shanti was anxious for the first time in her life because now she was too old to start looking for a new place. Moreover, she could only afford a place which would be too far out for her to walk to work. But Mohan Ram, who was a distant nephew, rallied a few people together and they took her to the patwari, the local official responsible for land records. He found that her uncle had built the house encroaching on land that belonged to the government and so it could not be sold. Shanti was relieved that once again luck was on her side.

* * *

A monkey was sitting alone beside a tree. When a few of us from the village passed that way, on our way to Gurur, it decided to follow us, walking a few paces behind. We were apprehensive that it might leap at any moment to snatch something and hurt us in the process. We tried to shake it off using threatening tones and

even by throwing a stone or two, but it would not go away.

As we neared an isolated hamlet, a dog began to bark and suddenly the monkey leapt up and clung to Tara Dutt's neck, quivering with fright. Tara was jolted and scared and tried to pull it off, but the monkey clung on with desperation. Tara realized that the monkey was more scared than him and attempted to stroke it gently. Only then did it leap off his back and resume its measured pace behind us until we came to the forest, where it bounded off.

* * *

Mohini Devi had a toothache, which lasted several days. Tara Dutt, her husband, watched helplessly as there was no dentist in the area, and there was no money to take her to the city.

Mohini could no longer bear the pain and she was ready to do anything to get the tooth out. She took her scythe and dug it in the ground and pressed the handle against her tooth with all her strength. The effort of it all seemed to distract her from the pain as she pushed and pushed, till the tooth loosened from the roots and fell out in a stream of blood. She collapsed, murmuring that hopefully now there would be an end to the pain.

Tara Dutt gave her cloves and pills to help soothe her pain. But he himself was plunged in depression, for he felt completely helpless. Pills and potions would not help his despondency, only his resolve would.

*   *   *

People in these remote villages have only a few consumer products in their homes, brought back by members of the family working in the plains. These are available for all to use, be it a lantern, an umbrella, a shawl or a chair for the occasional visitor.

Sometimes people who borrow these things break them, lose them or just keep them for months. People usually do not get unduly ruffled, as they know that when they need these things, they can get them back or borrow them from someone else. And if not, it is always possible to make do with a wick for a light, a plastic sheet in the rain or a rug to sit on the ground.

On the other hand, I am very attached to my knick-knacks, which have become an integral part of my personality. And, for fear of breakage, I hardly ever use them or let anyone borrow them.

*   *   *

Dewan Joshi had come home on a well-deserved rest after the rigorous time at the front in Kargil. But now he is involved with work in the village as his wife's sister, Kiran Devi, is to be married into this village. The parents of both the groom and the bride expect him to play an important role in the discussions and preparations for the wedding.

His friend, Puran Negi, too, is home from his new job in Chandigarh and wants to take Krishna and the children on a pilgrimage to Badrinath. But his cousin's daughter is to be married next spring and he has been invited by the in-laws-to-be, living in the village just beyond the ridge, to attend a Bhagwat Puja which will go on for a few days. Considering that negotiations are at a delicate stage, he has no option but to go, and Krishna quietly complies.

Both Dewan and Puran did not have much leave, but everyone agrees that it has been well spent.

*   *   *

Nature is moody here in the monsoon. Sometimes we wake up to bright blue skies, sometimes to a gentle mist over the valley and sometimes to dark clouds enveloping the whole range of mountains and, at times, storms streaking the sky with thunder and lightning.

The crested black tit and the tiny cinnamon tree sparrow adapt to these moods, splashing in the rain, huddling together in the trees in a storm, sitting motionless on overhead wires in a thick mist or flitting about in the sunshine.

I often sit and reminiscence about sunshine days and do not see the feathery mist as it floats over the valley or the grandeur of the thunder as it roars through the sky.

*   *   *

Tara Dutt's elder brother Manoj had been feeling uneasy for days. He knew that he should rest, because he felt out of breath even when fetching a bucket of water for the buffalo. But after days of inactivity, he could not resist the temptation of going with other retired army friends for his monthly ration of rum.

He walked slowly up the hill, and the companionship of his old comrades made him forget his physical condition. However, while returning home, he began to gasp with pain and could not proceed further. His friends carried him home and he seemed to revive as he drank tea with his family. But by evening, he began to breathe heavily again and in an inaudible voice whispered to his wife, Devaki Devi, 'I should not have risked the climb, for I have not yet got our daughters, Renu and Bhagvati, married.' And by nightfall he had 'gone away', as they say here, for death is not permanent, but a step in the journey beyond.

Everyone said that fate had decreed the time allotted to him, which could not have been extended, whether or not he had climbed the hill. The incident was but a pretext, and if not this then something else would have taken him away.

*   *   *

Through the silence of the night there is a cry, an invocation. In moments, the cry is taken up by others and there are voices all around. The village awakens and men and women run towards the house where death has been announced.

Women surround Devaki Devi as she wails in sorrow and misery for her husband. Her plight is brought home when Mohini Devi, her sister-in-law, moves forward and breaks her red bangles and removes her small gold nose ring to scrape off a thin sliver to be burnt with the body of her husband. The women can no longer hold back their sobs and even the men have tears in their eyes. Renu and Bhagvati, the daughters, cower petrified in a corner.

The men gather to discuss all that needs to be done and everyone contributes what they can for the expenses. Somebody runs to the local market to buy the white cloth to wrap the body and the red material for draping on top. Others arrange for transport to the burning-ghat and for ceremonies at the temple. A few begin to make the bier from bamboo obtained from the clump across the ridge.

Someone calls out that the bus has arrived. There is grief writ on all faces and loud laments from the women as the men set out on the last journey, taking turns as pallbearers. Manoj is given his final farewell at the temple like his forefathers before him.

Devaki could not think or move for a few days for

she was benumbed with the thought that the life shared so closely had gone and she was now alone.

* * *

It will be days before Devaki Devi's parents and brothers, in their remote hamlet, get the news of her husband's death. The ceremonies are already over and people have gone back home. Devaki sits in desolation behind the house, where the sun brings some warmth. Renu and Bhagvati scramble and run around, oblivious to the fact that the tumult and turmoil of yesterday was a prelude to a sadness which will overshadow their lives.

Neighbours and friends come to help. From the house below, Krishna Devi appears with a load of wood, which she puts down quietly in the courtyard. Panuli Devi calls out to the girls to come and eat, and in a little while, Mohini Devi places a plate of rice and dal near Devaki. She pushes the food away and her glazed eyes flicker ever so slightly.

Her immeasurable sorrow has confined her to her own world, which is out of reach to others. It is as if time is held in abeyance till she is ready to grasp the reality that awaits her.

* * *

Today is Janmasthami, the birthday of Lord Krishna. The children have been sent to buy a shirt, vest or something new for themselves; also, to purchase sugar and gram flour to make special sweets. Everyone is transformed from their casual appeareance with fancy clothes preserved for such occasions.

Chores are set aside as people gather together to go to the fair in the little town. Roadside stalls have sprung up overnight selling shiny beads and bangles, noisy toys and colourful balloons. The sweetmeat stalls with jalebis and spicy pakoras attract large crowds. Everyone is in a mood to spend a little on small things, just for merriment and delight.

I decided not to take time off from work to go to the festival, until I overheard them saying that I did not enjoy fun things.

*   *   *

After a death, many ceremonies and rituals have to be followed by close family members with an austere regimen of purification for eleven days. Baths have to be taken daily in the cold stream, special food has to be cooked by the mourners themselves, and several hours spent with priests for prayers and rituals.

When Kesar Dutt died, his cousin Tara Dutt could not go to the funeral as he had just lost his brother. And Kesar had no sons and only one brother, Gopal, with whom there was no contact. There were some cousins and a few old uncles who came for a day or two but they could not give the time for all that had to be done.

So Kamla Devi, his widow, had to undertake all

the rituals, which she somehow went through. But when the priest, bypassing the shaving of the head necessary for men, was ready to cut off her hair—which like other women she had tended ever since she could remember—she was overcome with grief.

Moved by her plight, Tara, who respected her husband, came immediately to fill in for the rest of the rites. The people in the village, too, had regard for Kesar, and came forward to help with the arrangements to feed the mourners at the final ceremony. This would enable Manoj to enter the next world without being indebted to anyone.

*   *   *

Early in the morning, before the day's work begins, Tara Dutt walks to the hill behind his fields and plants two oak saplings. This he has done every year during the monsoons for the last thirty years, as a quiet mission of his own. Now there is a virtual oak forest and still he continues his quest, unmindful of recognition.

*   *   *

Krishna Devi, though heavily pregnant, goes to the forest to collect wood while Shankar and Girdhar, her two small sons, play outside Mohini Devi's house. She stops for a moment and says, loud enough for just Mohini to hear, that she is going to the forest, as there is no fuelwood to cook food. Mohini says nothing but brings out a roti each for Krishna's boys. Now and again, she shouts at them when they are in her way and they scamper away like frightened mice only to start their childish antics again.

When Krishna returns with her load of wood, they follow her, clamouring for attention. Mohini stops for a moment and exchanges a smile with Krishna and each one then continues with her work.

Forgetting the usual formalities, I turned to my neighbours for help in a difficult situation. Their generous response lifted our casual relationship to a friendship of warmth and concern.

* * *

Krishna Devi called out to Pyari, and the cow ambled down the hill where she had been left to graze. She received an affectionate pat and on hearing the word '*gote*' went obediently into the dark, airless cowshed. Krishna gave her water, hay and two wheat-flour rotis that she had saved after the family meal. Pyari seemed to understand the caring gesture behind this tiny morsel.

Every morning, Krishna goes to cut fresh green grass and gives it to Pyari as soon as she brings her out from the gote. And only after that does Krishna drink her glass of tea. Then she cleans the gote and takes out the pine-needle bed dripping with dung and urine, and dumps it on the manure heap. She replaces it with fresh dry pine needles, which makes a warm, dry bed for Pyari. Later, when the sun is up, she walks with her to the stream at the edge of the field and gives her a good scrub. And then she makes a smoke fire of pine needles near where Pyari is tethered, so that mosquitoes and insects do not bother her.

Krishna's husband, Puran Negi, who has been away on a job in Chandigarh, has at long last got accommodation for her and the children and anxiously awaits their arrival. But Krishna cannot go, as she has not found a home that she considers good enough for Pyari. Everyone understands that, for, after all, her children have been raised on Pyari's milk.

Krishna gives Pyari almost the same consideration and care that she does to the family. It is difficult to find someone else who will give the same kind of love.

*   *   *

There was concern in the village because a few buffaloes and cows had got *khurpak*—foot and mouth disease. And when Tara Dutt's calf succumbed to the disease after two days of high fever and Hyat Joshi's buffalo died despite his efforts to treat it with local herbs, there was panic. People approached officials at the block office who said that they could not help, as the medicines were out of stock.

I contacted officials from the livestock department in the district, and, after a little persuasion, they arrived with phenyl, camphor, potassium and bandages. People were advised to isolate the sick animals and to feed them only green grass for fodder, but no grains or crop residue. With all these precautions, the disease was controlled and prevented from spreading, which brought relief all around.

*   *   *

The spider has woven its diaphanous web and waits patiently for its prey. The bees fly from the sunflowers to the hive in the awning of the unused shed. The snails slide unnoticed from the large puddle of water onto the smooth stone in the sun. And threadlike worms burrow and wriggle in the mud.

These small creatures live out their lives conforming to the inborn impulse of their species.

We live and act in accordance with our own thinking,

but explain away our straying as an inherent frailty of the human species.

*   *   *

Krishna Devi woke up with a feeling of discomfort but she knew it would be hours before her child was born. So she went to the fields to join the other women who were planting paddy saplings. Every now and again the pain would make her stop work. She would straighten up and stand for a few moments in the muddy water before bending down again to catch up with the rest as they planted row after row to cover the plot.

She caught sight of Tara Dutt, who was on his way to the adjoining village, and called out to him to send Madhavi Devi. After a while she left the others and walked up the hill to wait at her doorstep for Madhavi. When Madhavi arrived, both women went into the house and only Madhavi's deep low voice was audible as she sat behind Krishna, urging her to push as she massaged her back dextrously. In half an hour, the cry of the newborn announced that all was well.

Puran Negi, still in Chandigarh, got Tara Dutt's telegram after a few days and was delighted with the news of his newborn daughter—after all, he already had two sons. He rushed off to distribute sweets to his friends.

*   *   *

Puran Negi at long last commanded respect in the village, because he had a job in a factory. But he was in two minds about staying on, as he felt that it was right to be with his family, who could not leave the village to join him in Chandigarh. But now he had no choice as Krishna was having problems after the birth of their daughter. He would have to keep his job, for he was aware that the lack of facilities in the village could spell disaster for a helpless, sick woman.

He managed to get a month's leave, but as Krishna's condition continued to be unstable, he could not think of taking her with him to long journey to Chandigarh. Nor could he leave her behind in that state. So he stayed on in the village, and after three months when he went back, his explanations fell on deaf ears and his employers sacked him.

Puran was unsuccessful in finding another job, as he was not qualified enough. He had no option but to return to the village and resume work in his neighbours' fields. People felt that he was foolish to have given up a good job, since someone or the other would have taken care of his wife. But Puran said, 'My life would have no meaning without Krishna and I have no regrets.'

I have been trained to look for practical solutions and to find a place there for my idealism. But most people in this village start from the ideal and, if necessary, sacrifice the practical benefits.

* * *

Like all the others in the village, Devaki Devi grows wheat and rice in her fields. She keeps just a small patch for onions, garlic and a few green vegetables, barely enough for the needs of her small family. One day, her daughter Renu came up with an armful of fresh spinach for us. We were loath to accept Devaki's generous gift, until we learnt that being recently widowed she could not eat leafy vegetables, onions and garlic for a year.

There was also an unwritten code of dress, and she couldn't wear bright colours or any jewellery, or even the bangles that she had worn since childhood; moreover, she could not participate in any ceremonies or celebrations during the mourning period. But she did have the joy of visits from neighbours who would come and talk with her in the evenings, after their work in the fields. This was enough for Devaki; she did not demand anything more of her neighbours and friends.

* * *

The *akas-bel*, a local vine, grew innocuously on the ground but soon it wound itself round the oak tree, drawing succour from its bark. Gradually it detached itself from the dry earth, and the oak became its sole source of survival. It grew thick, strong branches, which entangled themselves with the branches of the oak, threatening to strangle it. People then hacked it away to save the oak.

Sometimes dependence grows imperceptibly, crushing one's individuality and also affecting the lives of those who set out to help.

* * *

Hira Joshi, Dewan's young son, walks behind his father as he ploughs the field, and learns to sow the seeds in furrows (unlike his father's father, who most probably scattered the seeds in the field and let nature take its course). Bishan Kathayat plants fruit saplings and cardamom root slips that he has brought from the plains. And Tara Dutt has replaced yam and gourds with cauliflower and peas, for these sell better to tourists who visit in the summer. Other farmers show interest in these changes and gradually new crops appear in the village.

I draw upon the wisdom of past generations and the knowledge and learning of people today. But I like to believe that whatever I do is with my own effort.

* * *

Kundan Kathayat's son Prem was returning from the market with a heavy sack of wheat that he and his friend were carrying by turns. He was in a happy mood, laughing and joking with his friend, because his marriage had been arranged for the following month; in fact, the wheat had been bought to feed the guests.

Just then a bus came by and Prem moved distractedly to the edge of the road to let it pass. He lost his balance on a slippery stone and went hurtling down to the stream. He lay stunned for a few seconds and got up startled to see the wheat scattered along the hillside. His friend ran down to help him and was much relieved to find that Prem had gotten away with minor bruises and scratches.

Prem limped home, while his friend carried a lighter sack with the remnants of the wheat. Kundan and his wife, Rekha Devi, were shaken at the thought of what could have happened to their son and went to the temple in thankful prayer. But a few hours later, Kundan, backed by his brother Bishan, went into a tirade about Prem's careless behaviour and raved and ranted about the loss of wheat.

Even after major concerns have been resolved, why are we not content? Why do we start ferreting out minor issues to worry about?

*   *   *

Nand Bahadur is totally dependent on daily-wage labour as he has no land or other means of income. His only asset is his physical strength and his trademark is his thick, strong rope, slung across his shoulder to bind the heavy loads he carries on his back. He is quiet and humble when he speaks to the farmers and shopkeepers who employ him. At the end of the day he waits for his payment, standing respectfully, or sitting on the ground, while they discuss the day's business over a cup of tea.

But when he comes home he has a swaggering gait, as he calls out to Mamta Devi, his wife, in a lordly manner. His children, Indra and Pappu, dart around, putting away his shoes and bringing him water, while his wife prepares tea. He describes the day's happenings and tells Mamta how a shopkeeper persuaded him to lift a heavy load that no one else could carry.

I move up and down the status ladder in relation to the society in which I find myself. But still I do not concede that these rankings are transitory.

*　*　*

Rekha Devi discovered that her paddy saplings were dying because someone had disconnected her water supply. She was sure that it was Manoj Dutt's widow, Devaki Devi, who was in constant need of water for her vegetable patch, her buffaloes and her household. That evening she complained to her husband, Kundan Kathayat, about Devaki, and together they raged and ranted about her and the wrongdoings of her family. They recalled how their grandfather was assaulted because Devaki's family wanted to wrest a piece of his land, bordering their fields. All this got Rekha very worked up and she said that she would pull out the pipes conveying water and, if necessary, let her fields remain dry along with Devaki's fields. But she would not tolerate this harrassment.

The next morning Rekha went to the fields only to find that even Devaki's patch was dry. In fact, it was farmers further downstream who had crept up and disconnected all the pipes as they were transplanting paddy. So Rekha and Devaki decided to watch for the real culprits . . . and deep family disputes were buried once again.

They had a tenuous and uncertain friendship, because they could not shed the burdensome memories of their difficult relationship in the past.

*   *   *

Every home has a shrine, be it just a tiny alcove with a small statue of Vishnu, Shiv, Parvati or Bhairav Nath. It is part of the daily life of people to pray there, at least once a day, to seek comfort and support, or in thankfulness. When the little bells ring out and the conch sounds, people know that the household is at prayer.

Every now and then someone holds a yagna, when gods are propitiated for a special boon—be it for the birth of a son, the neutralizing of a troublesome sprite or in gratitude for a wish granted. The beats of the dhol and *dhanua*, the large and small drums, reverberate rhythmically all day. Everyone in the village and in the neighbourhood responds to the call and takes part in the ceremony. As Vijay Joshi, who is respected for his views, said, 'The prayer and faith we share is what matters in our life. The rest is mere existence.'

My faith is something more personal and does not find a clear tangible expression. When they were growing up, my children would question, 'Where is God', and I would tell them, 'I am searching.' Now, after years, they, too, have learnt that the quest is a necessary part of the understanding.

* * *

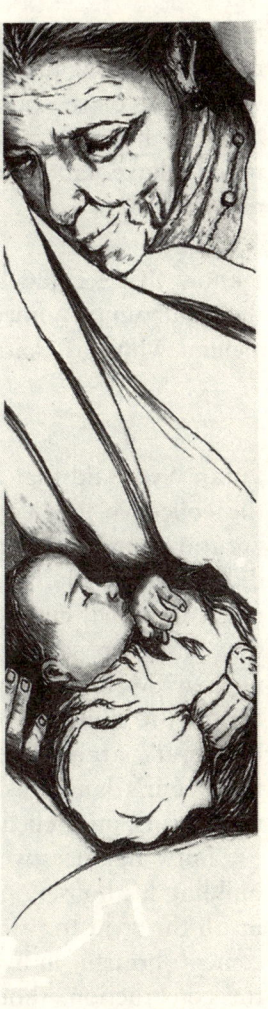

Govindi Devi walks bent over a stick, carrying her frayed cushion from place to place to catch the sun as it moves. She talks to herself, half aloud, so that anyone who cares can listen to forgotten episodes, travails and joys.

After sunset she moves indoors near the kitchen fire, smoking her hookah and taking in the family. She listens to them, talking of the day's events, of Hansi's forthcoming marriage, about the quarrel with the neighbours over water and of the good wheat crop. Her mind drifts away to her own past as she mumbles in a muffled tone, 'I have had a rich life and all my family is here to prove it.'

I know that I could live my retirement in comfort in the community home. Only, there would be nobody around who has shared my past.

*   *   *

Puran Negi said that it was unfair to pay his share of the collective municipal water tax, because he had a natural source of water in his own field. Vijay Joshi did not want the women to go across his fields to reach the chaff-cutter on the other side, as he feared that his crop would be trampled. Panram and his nephew Mohan Ram vied with each other for the contract to build the local school. The fact that Bishan Kathayat's grandfather had usurped a section of his neighbour's land was brought up every time the two neighbours quarrelled.

But differences were set aside when Tara Dutt was building his house: one woman from each family went up to the road to bring down head-loads of brick and cement, brought in by truck. The men were engaged in the construction, shouting advice to each other.

It was the same during Chandra's wedding when everyone in the village pitched in to cook, to decorate her home or to take care of the groom's party. Maybe this working together can be explained away as a necessity for survival, but it does bring goodwill and fun all around.

*   *   *

Bishan Kathayat's second daughter, Hansi, is getting married and preparations are underway. The bark of the *kaphal* and *utis* trees collected from the forest is drying in the sun. This will provide the rust-and-yellow colour for decorating the house for the wedding. Sacks of rice and wheat begin to pile up in the kitchen. The whole village has to be fed as well as some guests from other villages—over 200 people in all. And there are two sacks of coconuts to be distributed to all the guests.

Word has gotten around and the wandering trader who treks from village to village has arrived with a stack of saris, for it is a part of the ritual to give saris to members of the family and special guests.

There is also the suit for the groom and a shimmering sari for the bride, who will also get the traditional jewellery which every bride gets, as well as an extra gold bracelet, in keeping with her father's status.

Bishan has saved for years for his daughter's wedding, keeping a tight control on all household expenses—though his son Kailash's requirements were an exception. Even for the wedding, his wife, Panuli Devi, will wear the sari given to her by his brother Kundan during his son Prem's wedding. They both agree that there should be no unnecessary expenditure but only that which will give them respect and standing in the community.

* * *

Panuli Devi stands out as the mother of the bride in her bright green sari and an orange overcloth with red polka dots, fringed with gold tassels, worn only at family weddings and ceremonies. Besides the jewellery usually worn on festive occasions, she wears the beautiful old *nath*, the gold nose ring handed down from her mother-in-law, who remembers it being in the family for two generations before her.

The wedding guests have just finished their afternoon meal and everyone is engrossed in singing and dancing. While the women from the village start the preparations for tea, Panuli puts away the decorative overcloth and removes her nath. She wraps it carefully in an old cloth, ties it around her waist and slips out to the pond. She brings two buckets of water for the cattle in the gote and gives them green grass cut earlier in the day, before proceeding to milk the cow. As the animals are used to her, no one else does these jobs. After a while she emerges, transformed again as the mother of the bride.

In the afternoon, the women get down to preparing the feast for the evening. While the young girls are deployed to knead the mounds of flour for the puris, the men are engaged in constructing the pandal where all the gifts will be displayed.

*   *   *

The weeks of preparation were exciting for Hansi, who, as the bride, was the centre of attention. At sixteen years of age, it was overwhelming to be given lovely clothes, jewellery, fancy furniture and even a vanity case. And to be carried in a doli right up to the main road.

Now, the village must bid her farewell. Although the thought of leaving home is sad, at least she still has her younger brother, Kailash, and Prem, her uncle Kundan's son, who will be accompanying the baraat to take her to her new home . . .

Only when it was time for Prem and Kundan to leave would panic have gripped her, as she would have realized that she was left in the midst of people she did not know at all. She had only seen her husband during the ceremony and had not even spoken to him. At that moment, all the excitement of the wedding would have meant nothing compared to the sense of loss that she must have felt.

Thinking of her, I was reminded of the time when I was away from home, and a breach in the road made

my return uncertain. I could no longer savour the
excitement and adventure of my new surroundings.
My only concern was to get back home.

*   *   *

The proliferating weed with its tall straggling stem and
purple flowers grows along the edge of fields. Farmers
call it *besharam*, that which is without shame, because
when not controlled it spreads recklessly into the
fields. They don't bother about it till it is time to sow
the fields and then they labour and toil to remove it
from the very roots.

I brush aside my troubles till they multiply in the face
of my indifference and begin to impinge upon my life,
and I can no longer look away.

*   *   *

Mohini Devi, who worked as a schoolteacher, was cut
to the quick when Panram mentioned in the presence
of others that her uncle had only one eye. Even though
he had lost it on the battlefield as a young soldier, she
felt sure that people would interpret it to be a retribution
for a sinful life, be it a previous one.

Mohini could not take this insult to her family and
avoided going past Panram's house, even though it
now took her half an hour longer to get to school.

She read hidden meanings in his harmless remarks,

reflecting her own vulnerability. This caused needless heartache.

*   *   *

Ever since she was widowed, Devaki Devi has been very hard-pressed for time. The women in the village talk about her unkempt children and say that she should give more attention to them.

But today Devaki has taken time off from the fields to bathe Renu and Bhagvati. She brings out a bucket of hot water and strips them in the warm sun, soaping and scrubbing them. There are squeals of delight intermingled with whimpering as the cool wind chills them and the soap gets into their eyes.

As they dry themselves in the sun, Devaki brings out their clothes, some too large, some too small and hanging askew. But the girls look cherubic and fresh as they run off to play. And Devaki hurries to work in the fields.

She has set her priorities, which fit into her scheme of things, even though they seem off-balance to others.

*   *   *

The incessant rain saturated the soil, making it soggy and marshy. The flooded stream rushed down the hillside, spilling over into the fields. The water dripped from the canopy of trees on to the vegetable patch. The buffalo strained at the wooden post and, cutting loose from its rope, wallowed down the slippery, wet hillside.

The birds perched on the roof cleaned and spruced themselves, flicking the raindrops from their wings. The purple-winged butterflies bathed in raindrops and drank nectar from the flowers.

My grandchildren, who are visiting me, splash happily in the mud and rain, unmindful of the wet and cold. I am anxious for them and cannot dwell on the fragrance of the rain on the parched dry fields, or on the fresh green beauty of the trees after their shower.

*   *   *

Hansi, the new bride, was sweeping the house carefully, the way she had been taught by her mother, Panuli Devi. Her mother-in-law watched her quietly while washing the utensils. She wanted to make sure that she had a good daughter-in-law, so she had thrown a rupee coin unobtrusively under the bed. If the coin remained there, then her new daughter-in-law was not a good worker and if the coin was not there and not returned, then she could not be trusted.

Fortunately for Hansi, her mother had warned her that it was necessary to be very cautious, especially in the first few days, until her new family relaxed with the stranger in their midst. She did see the gleaming coin in the corner behind the bedpost and somehow knew that it had been placed there. She felt humiliated but picked it up quietly and put it near the deity in the alcove, and went outside, away from her mother-in-law, into the fresh air.

* * *

The peach tree is laden with fruit and myriad leaves, all of which have come from one seed. In this marvel of growth, not one peach, nor indeed one leaf, is exactly the same size and shape. Nor would we want it so.

I did my best to chisel and mould my daughters into the models I wanted. But they sprouted their own individuality, their own specialness that baffled and sometimes frustrated me.

* * *

The heavy monsoon rain turned the gentle rippling stream into a raging torrent. The farmers feared that the crops of chillies, ginger and turmeric would be flooded and damaged. So they got together and built a *bund*—a small dam—across the stream, but no one wanted to give a strip of land to channel the overflow.

The constant rain over three days accumulated water right up to the brim of the bund, and since there was no channel for the overflow, the pressure of water cut into the bund. Water flooded the fields, carrying with it the standing crop.

I was disappointed, and it was a while before I

realized that I was being unfair in expecting the people of the village to be always perfect.

*   *   *

Rekha Devi and Devaki Devi had always been in competition and would look for any excuse to fight. In the dry summer months, they would claim that the other had dislodged the pipe conveying water from the stream. During the monsoon, they would hurl accusations at each other for cutting grass from the other's field. In the winter, each would allege that branches had been hacked for firewood from the other's trees.

The fight spilled over to the children. One day Rekha caught Devaki's daughter Bhagvati plucking her pears and just throwing them around. She threatened her with dire consequences if she caught her at it again. In retaliation the young girl shook her own pear tree, which overhung Rekha's paddy fields, scattering the large green pears over ripening paddy fields, crushing the plants.

Although Rekha usually avoided contact with Devaki, this time she confronted her. But, as usual, Devaki denied Bhagvati's role in any mischief and said that the pears fell with the strong wind earlier in the day. Nothing that Rekha said could make a dent in Devaki's unflinching stand that her daughter was innocent. Rekha, in exasperation, said that she would put some of the broken paddy stalks in the temple of

Golu Maharaj, the god of justice. And then if Bhagvati was guilty, she would not be responsible for any retribution. But if the girl was innocent, Devaki need not worry.

Whereupon Devaki, forgetting her stand, shouted and screamed at Rekha for even thinking of such a punishment for her daughter just for the sake of a few paddy stalks.

Bhagvati knew that she could always count on her mother's unequivocal support in any situation. This had given her the freedom to act without restraint, and I worried for her.

* * *

Nobody knows how old Govindi Devi is, and even her son Bishan is not quite sure. She has always been there as far as anybody can remember. But now age has taken its toll and her body aches in the chill and damp of the monsoon. She takes the medicines she is given, but says, 'It will not help as I do not have many days left.'

She demands nothing, not even a visit from her other son, Kundan, who is away in the plains, and says, 'If he comes, it is fine; if not, it does not matter.' She speaks without anguish or anxiety, merely stating the truth as she feels it. She has seen two generations go before her and there are three generations here with her. But she is bound to the past; the present can no longer hold her and she is ready to go.

* * *

The Board Examination was to be held in the village of Chanauda, which had a suitably large hall. Also, being away from the local school, there would be no chance of the children copying and cheating. This meant that children from the villages five to ten kilometres around had to commute the distance every day, getting up early to catch the bus, to be on time for the first paper.

But Vijay Joshi's brother Hyat said that he was lucky to have relatives living there, for his brother-in-law's daughter was married in that village. The family had kindly agreed to keep Sunder, his grandson, for the period of the exams. Moreover, being teachers, they had even offered to help him with his studies.

With the tempo of life in the city, one can barely keep in touch with immediate family and close friends. And regretfully one loses out on meaningful relationships with the extended family.

*   *   *

The torrent rushes down the mountain, crashing against stones along the side, circling around huge boulders and carrying pebbles for miles downstream. Over the years the boulders and stones lose their sharp edges and take on beautiful rounded shapes, dappled with various hues of granite. But the rocks beyond the river remain grey and jagged, as they always were.

I have chosen the quiet of the shore but every now and then, the flow and tide of events pulls me into the fray, which helps to plane down at least some of the rough edges that I unwittingly develop in my isolation.

*   *   *

There are sixty-five children in the village primary school with classes from the first to the fifth standard. Although there are two teachers, often one of them is assigned duties for collecting various official data, to assist in local elections or medical camps, to arrange for rations given to children of backward classes and other such tasks. The one teacher there moves from one distracted group to another and as a result the lessons are disjointed and disrupted. The village elders, though concerned, were unwilling to teach the children themselves, and put forward the lack of time as an excuse.

But Vijay Joshi, who is particular about childrens' education, has asked Sunita Devi, his daughter-in-law who has passed high school, to coach all the children who come to the house in the evening. She sits in the courtyard with earnest faces around her and painstakingly goes through the lessons. The little ones struggle with the alphabet, repeating slowly after her and forming letters on their slates. The slightly older children read haltingly until, at last, the lesson is mastered. And Hira, Sunder and other ten-year-olds pour over arithematic problems.

* * *

Bishan Kathayat's daughter Hansi had come home from her in-laws, but the once cheerful, smiling face was now careworn. Slowly the picture of her new life emerged: 'Yes, my husband is kind and doing well, as my father found out before settling the match. But he lives in Delhi and comes home only once a year for a few weeks.

'My mother-in-law runs the home and she believes that daughters-in-law should not sit around but be active all day with something or the other, which she can always find for us to do. My sister-in-law and I leave the house at sunrise after eating one or two rotis, kept aside from last night's dinner, to collect firewood from the distant forest. We come home after three hours and immediately start cooking the morning meal for which our mother-in-law has prepared only the rice. And then, if there is no fieldwork, we set out for another head-load of wood, even though our courtyard is stacked high with enough wood for a year, some of it rotting.

'Sometimes my sister-in-law and I sit in the forest and talk of our families, our lives as children and of people in the village. It makes us laugh and also weep—and somehow we feel better. On our return we have to bring several buckets of water from the tap further up from our house and then get down to cooking the evening meal.

'No, I have not told my parents about my new life. They can do nothing, they have to live in the community. Why make them suffer? This is my karma, and I have to live with it.' And she turned her face away. She was burdened with a life not really of her choice, and sadly she was not equipped to find her own way.

*   *   *

The school bell sounded across the hill, but Munni ran in the opposite direction, towards Dewan Joshi's house. She asked his son Hira for some cow's urine, in which nettle leaves are soaked and used for purification. This was necessary because her mother, Mohini Devi, had her monthly period and had to be 'separate'. If Munni or her cousin Bhagvati or indeed any visitor touched her mother accidentally, then the wet nettle would be sprinkled on them.

Hira adeptly lifted the cow's tail and rubbed her flanks gently to procure the urine.

The school bell sounded again and Hira rushed off, leaving Munni to amble home to do the cooking because her mother could not enter the kitchen.

People hold on to beliefs decreed by revered elders for reasons relevant to their times. No doubt the wise, always ahead of their time, would have themselves shed outworn and sometimes corrupted doctrines.

*   *   *

The monsoon brings much awaited succour to the parched brown earth. But it also brings some unwelcome visitors who find their way into the house by mysterious routes: snails slide into the smooth cooking pans; insects find their way into the wheat bin; beetle-like airborne creatures buzz around the light in the room.

But it is the large spider above the kitchen sink which bothers me, for despite my splashing it with water, it doesn't move an inch. It is there again the next day in exactly the same spot. I approach it gingerly to find it hanging lifeless on the wall supported by its sticky legs.

*   *   *

The sun is out after days of rain and a flock of little cinnamon tree sparrows sit twittering on the leafy branches of the peach trees. I scatter some seeds on the balcony and wait expectantly, but they continue to chirrup amongst themselves, seemingly unconcerned with my gesture.

After a while, when I tire of waiting and return to my newspaper, one bold creature flies gingerly to the balcony, takes a quick peck and flies back to the safety of the flock. It returns, looking from side to side with nervous, jerky movements, and moves cautiously to take a few more pecks. A rustle of the newspaper scares it and it flies off. In a while it returns again, and I scarcely breathe as it pecks away with increasing assurance. The others watching from the safety of the trees swoop down to join it, and soon there is only the tapping sound of busy beaks.

*　*　*

The plot of land on the far side of the village that has belonged to Bishan Kathayat's family for generations was a little distant from Bishan's main fields, and sometimes he could not even manage to plough it. So when Radha, his third daughter, was to get married and he needed money, he sold it to Hyat Joshi's son, Raghunath.

Raghunath, who was living in the city, had taken to drinking with his friends there, and over the years developed a liver problem. Eventually this took a serious turn, and the doctors could not save him. Raghunath died, leaving behind his widow, Janki Devi, and three daughters. Her brother-in-law, Jivan, in accordance with the prevailing practice, took proprietary interest in her land, offering to give Janki a part of the produce. However, Janki felt it was unfair that her land should be taken away just because she had no son. She was looking for a way out, when Kundan approached her to buy back the plot that his brother had sold; he was sentimental about the plot. Janki boldly agreed and sealed the deal before her brother-in-law could intervene. As she began to understand her legal rights, she felt more confident and asserted her claim over her share of the main family plots, too.

Jivan was furious at being outwitted and challenged by a 'mere woman' and tried to muster support in the village by producing Raghunath's statement, written just before he died. Although he had indeed said that the land should be divided between Jivan and his son Sunder, he had also said that they should take care of Janki and their three daughters. But it was hard for people to judge whether Jivan had not kept his part of the bargain, or whether Janki's conduct was responsible for the situation. With mixed opinions, no settlement could be reached and Janki took charge of her land— with the full support of her daughters—which indeed was her legal right.

I understood the villagers' dilemma. On many occasions when I have tried to bring about a rapproachement between two friends, both have had such a different perspective of the facts, that the truth has eluded me.

* * *

People have remained shut in and gloomy through the interminable dark, overcast monsoon days. Everyone is edgy for there is so much to be done in the fields and at home. Even the children no longer relish the enforced holiday.

The sun has remained hidden for days. But now there is a blush on the grey clouds, which seem embarrassed to have obstructed the sun. They hastily make way for it to emerge, and once again life takes on its tempo and people bustle about with renewed vitality.

*   *   *

This morning, Krishna Devi came to Mohini Devi's house to ask for a little cow's milk needed for the special prayer being offered to the family deity. After a while, Sunita Devi arrived saying that her son Hira was home from school and she wanted half a glass of cow's milk for his tea, as her cow had run dry; the rest of the family, like everybody else at such times, drank tea without milk. Mohini was already committed to selling most of the milk to clients in the bazaar, but all the same she doled out some of the milk that had been set aside for her own family's tea. She could not refuse her neighbours' requests, for one day she would be in a similar position when her cow ran dry.

By the time Manju Devi came up to ask for milk for her pregnant daughter-in-law, Mohini had really nothing to spare, so Manju offered to give some of her buffalo's milk in exchange for the cow's milk.

*   *   *

Puran Negi set out just before dawn, as he does each day, to go to the forest to gather a large head-load of wood to sell in the market. He was tired and worn after the steep climb and was glad to be rid of his heavy load but, much as he wanted to, he did not stop in the market for a cup of tea that would have cost him two rupees. When he got home, he gratefully drank the steaming glass of tea which his wife, Krishna Devi, had made for him, and ate two thick rotis.

After a few minutes' rest he set off to work on the tea estate to transplant saplings which had been sent from a distant nursery. He worked all day, with a short break for lunch, for which he went back home. Krishna could not bring the food for him, because their little daughter was still too young to be left alone, and also because she had to tend their little vegetable plot.

On returning home in the evening, Puran went off to deliver his neighbour's fruit to the market.

Puran's two sons, Shankar and Girdhar, left early for school and thereafter they had tuitions and homework. Puran was determined that, unlike him, they should be educated and find good jobs and, unlike others in the village, he deliberately did not involve them in work at home or in the forest or the tea estate. People felt sorry for him sometimes, and few even admired him.

One day, on his return from the market, Puran, who had stored his money in the rice sack, found that it had disappeared. He cried out desperately that now he could never build his house, for which he had saved for years; and nothing that anybody said could console him. Meanwhile, Krishna, who had been rummaging through the grain sack, discovered that the money had slipped further inside when she had hurriedly taken out the rice for the midday meal. Puran stood still for a moment and then let out a yelp of joy as he ran into the house.

Neighbours who had gathered there began to say that Puran was really better off than they had thought, for after all they could not even think of repairing their homes, leave alone building a new one. And although people still saw him trudging to the market with his daily load and rushing all day from one job to another, they were no longer sympathetic.

No one wanted to hear of the sacrifices and the immense effort made by him to get to his present position. It was just difficult to accept that he had reached where he had, and they had been left behind.

* * *

Panuli is up early, and along with her youngest daughter, Bhavna, starts on various chores for the day—sweeping the house, swabbing the kitchen with a mixture of red earth and cow dung, preparing the hookah for the old father-in-law and giving water to the buffalo.

When tea is ready for the household, she calls out to Kailash, 'Come son, it's time to get up.' She hurries back to the kitchen to help Bhavna finish her work there, before sending her to the fields to cut grass for fodder. But she goes back and forth, coaxing and urging Kailash to get up for the steaming tea that awaits him. Finally a weary response emanates from the room, and after some mutterings a drowsy Kailash emerges, groping for his glass of tea.

Panuli was steeped in traditional thinking and so treated her son and daughters differently, even though she loved them equally. She could not see the lifelong impact this would have on them.

*   *   *

Kasti Devi never mentioned her marriage, which was in the distant past. People spoke of a drunken husband and cruelty that forced her to return to her maternal home. Her brothers Bishan and Kundan Kathayat accepted her back and she ate on alternate days with each brother, sharing a room with Govindi Devi, her old mother. She spent her time taking care of her mother and helping her sisters-in-law with the work in the field and home. Her one joy was to spend a few days each year with her married sister who lived in a village four to five hours away.

Govindi had been ailing for years and gradually her condition worsened, so much so that she could not even move out of bed without help. Kasti's whole day and sometimes even nights were taken up with nursing her mother. Everybody felt that Kasti was the only person who had the time to do so and as a result, she could not leave the house, not even to visit her sister. At times she could not contain her frustration and muttered about her sisters-in-law and the demands of Govindi. It was especially hard in winter when she had to carry all the bedclothes to the stream to wash them clean in the freezing cold or to light the fire late at night when her mother wanted tea.

Govindi was particularly cheerful that fateful morning, for her grandson had carried her out in the sun. She lay there hearing the voices of the young children playing around her. But that night she began to breathe heavily and asked Kasti to send for her sons. Even as they clambered up the steps to the room, Govindi closed her eyes and breathed her last.

Although Govindi's death had been expected for months, the suddenness of it shook the family and especially Kasti. All the years of misery were forgotten and she could only repeat that the house was empty and now there was nothing for her to do.

Govindi had become difficult and imperious as she grew older, but when she died, rancour and hurt receded, leaving her family with the anguish of her absence and the nostalgia of joyful moments.

* * *

Mahal, the wild pear tree, is grafted with a local cultivated pear variety. The grafted tree does not need care, no hoeing, weeding, fertilizer or irrigation, but grows on its own like its wild parent. In about three years, it yields fruit, which, unlike delicate table pears, peaches and plums, is hard and solid and does not fetch a good price. But when peaches and plums are battered by hailstorms, the wild pear survives with its resilience and can be transported to the plains. This lowly pear is then a buttress for the farmers.

I had expected that my affectionate and caring daughters would be my support and strength in my old age. But I had not bargained for the love and concern I have received from my nephew, the 'black sheep' of the family. He had seemed so vulnerable and weak, but emerged unexpectedly strong and dependable.

*   *   *

The paddy crop, fresh and vitalized with the monsoon rain, sways gently in the wind and the tousled heads of the *mandua*—millet—bow with the weight of its coarse grain. But now, with over two months of rain, the ripening grain needs the sun. More rain could flatten the heavily laden plants, so the farmers are praying for days of clear sunshine.

The monsoon, which has been propitiated and blessed, is reluctant to leave. Since the last two days, it has flashed with rage and bellowed thunderously because it is no longer welcome.

My grandchildren delighted in my coming and I basked in their attention. But with holidays over, they are engrossed with school and their classmates. My pace is no longer in rhythm with the tempo of their lives.

*   *   *

Devaki Devi's buffalo was old and could no longer give milk, but it still had to be fed, for it had given milk to the family all these years. This was a burden for Devaki, as being a widow with two school-going daughters, she had to do all the work in the house and in the fields. So she skimped on the grass for the old buffalo while giving a fair share to the two-year-old calf that would provide milk in two years' time. The buffalo began to look thin and starved and in time could barely stand. One day it sat listlessly with its head dangling on one side and it seemed that it would not last long. But Devaki had to go to the post office to collect her meagre pension and even though she hurried back, by the time she returned, the buffalo was already dead.

The women in the village said that they would never have starved a buffalo that had so faithfully given milk to the family. And on top of that, it was a crime not to have seen its face before it died.

We tend to impose our own perspectives on others less fortunate and more vulnerable, whose guiding factor is pure survival.

*   *   *

The sky is overcast and black clouds are moving towards the village. The heavy rain has caused breaches in the road, and trucks and buses can no longer operate. The farmers are waiting impatiently, for the bags of fruit and vegetables, ready for the market, are beginning to rot.

The women are anxious for there are no visitors from the plains to bring news of their sons working there. The children are sulking and squabbling with the forced confinement. The isolation of the village accentuated with the dark, wet days brings with it a sense of resignation and gloom.

*   *   *

For the last few days, the ear had got attuned to the sound of rain drumming on the tin roof. Last evening, in the fast fading light, we became conscious of the silence, even before we were aware that the rain had stopped. Other sounds surfaced: the gurgle and splash of the stream as it tumbled down the hill, the chirruping of birds settling down for the night, the monotonous call of the cicada and the rustling of an indiscernible animal.

The lights in the valley came alive and the clouds drifted away to reveal a canopy of stars. Wrapped in the unaccustomed quiet, I find thoughts buried away in my mind floating to the surface.

*   *   *

Ghuria was an ill-tempered bull and everyone skirted carefully past it, for even when it was tethered it lunged forward with a snort and gave people a fright. It would lock horns with the young bull near it and try to get at the fresh grass given to Bachi, the cow. When Mohini Devi's daughter Munni took it out to graze, it would disregard her and go into other people's fields and eat their vegetables or chase their cows. And Munni had to seek help from Dewan Joshi's son Hira to get Ghuria back into the shed.

But with Bachi's newborn calf, this big, burly bull showed unexpected tenderness. Ghuria would gently lick the calf as it scampered around playfully.

*   *   *

The deep mist that has settled over the valley rises slowly, enveloping all that is around us—hills, forests and hamlets vanish from sight. The distant sound of rain approaches nearer and nearer and before we know it, we are inundated in a deluge. Devaki Devi's voice, calling out to her daughter Renu, can no longer be heard. There is only the drumming of the rain accentuated by the flash of lightning and the crash of thunder.

People, reacting to the forces beyond them, start singing a ballad of the bravery and courage of a past hero and many join in the chorus. The voices melt into the symphony of the elements.

In the city, people reacted differently to the rain. The roads were flooded in the monsoon, the drains were clogged, cars and buses honked and umbrellas, like black mushrooms, sprouted everywhere. I used to be trapped in the traffic, frustrated and impatient like everyone else, wanting to get home.

*   *   *

There was a break in the monsoon rain, and I decided to go with a few women to a neighbouring village. We set off at dawn on the track that winds its way to the valley below. The soil had been washed away along the hillside, carrying with it boulders and plants that were now strewn across our path, which we negotiated with difficulty. In places, we had to climb over the trees which were uprooted and lay lifeless, blocking our way. Tiny streams trickled down, creating eddies and pools which splattered us with mud as we waded across regretting that we ventured out on this path. I was so engrossed with the difficulties of the journey that I missed the flight of birds in the young light of dawn.

The track wound its way through fields of tall maize and ripening paddy plants. School children with faces barely visible above the crops passed us in their bright blue uniforms, immersed in conversation. They moved about with ease, unmindful of the pitfalls and blockages, laughing delightedly as they splashed mischievously in the pools of water along the way.

*　*　*

The downpour and squall came with the rage of the retreating monsoon and the dark, dense clouds were pierced with knife-edged blades of light. The patter of rain on the tin roof turned into a torrential downpour, hurling large white hailstones recklessly in all directions. The anger of the skies mounted into a crescendo, drowning every other sound. It was only after the storm died down that I heard the song of the whistling thrush.

Often, I remember, it was the truth spoken quietly in the silent aftermath of an impassioned outburst that stayed with me, and not all the other words that had been shouted out.

*　*　*

Panuli Devi is up earlier than usual because her daughter Hansi is returning with her husband to her parents-in-law. She looks around in her small field to see what her daughter can take with her.

Panuli is still agile enough to climb the pear tree, for hidden in the thick creeper entwining it, there are six cucumbers. And on the vine trailing on the ground in the vegetable patch, she spots three pumpkins covered by large leaves. The maize crop has not been good due to the heavy rains, but she manages to find a few cobs that are edible. All this, together with some home-grown wheat and millet grains, fills up a reasonably large-sized gunny bag. Hansi will not go back empty-handed from her parents' home.

I was looking through my things to find something special for my granddaughter. Just then, she came running in from the garden to give me a daisy, crushed tightly in her little fist.

*   *   *

Every now and again, I can hear people calling out loudly from across their distant houses to each other or to the children who are grazing cattle in the far hills. I have become familiar with the nicknames of the children, especially the unruly ones, who respond reluctantly from some truant game. When Chandra got married and moved away to another village, I missed hearing 'Channa, Channa', as she was affectionately called by her mother, and her response 'Ooyee'—the colloquial for 'O, Mother'.

In her new home, Chandra did not hear her name any more, for she was merely addressed as 'bahu', or daughter-in-law. When her son was born, she became 'Dinesh's mother' to everyone, even her husband; and after a while, she was affectionately known as 'Dineshi'.

But she was joyful when she was back home and could hear 'Channa, Channa' resounding on the hillside.

When her aged brother died, my ninety-year-old aunt was lost in silent thought. Then, in a small voice, almost to herself, she said, 'Now I will not be anyone's kid sister and will no longer hear my childhood name.'

*   *   *

With the receding monsoon, women begin to prepare for the long, cold winter when food is limited and unvaried. In the courtyard of every household there are thalis filled with shredded radish and cucumber and chopped spinach and mustard, which are set out to dry in the subdued sunshine. The pumpkins are put in neat rows on the beam of the sloping roofs so that cows and buffaloes too would have something to supplement the dry hay in winter.

When Tara Dutt and Mohini Devi were away in the fields, a horde of monkeys came and settled on their roof to feast on the pumpkins and attacked the drying vegetables. Munni and the other children around shouted themselves hoarse but could not frighten the monkeys away and by the time the neighbours got to the scene, the feast was over and there was nothing left.

Tara Dutt was dismayed at first, but then he told his wife and neighbours that Hanuman, the monkey-god, was entitled to his share, and that they did have yams, potatoes, lentils and some fresh spinach for the winter.

Living in the remote hills, I realize that I do not miss the many things that I had considered so indispensable for my living. On the contrary, I find that they had weighed me down.

WINTER

The valley and the surrounding hills are barely discernible through the billowing mist. But now, like a candle lit by an invisible hand, there is a glow of soft-hued pink on Trishul, which stands out above the shadowy range. As the sun climbs up from behind the eastern range, the pink deepens to crimson and spills over the snow-clad mountains, which are aglow from end to end, from Chaukhama to Panchchuli.

The mist melts away like candyfloss, and the houses take shape. The green carpet now changed to brown for the winter is on display in the fields. The trees, sharp and clear, with bared arms, stand guarding the regal mountains in the horizon.

When the world before me can regain itself in just a few minutes, why do I harbour lingering shadows?

* * *

In the morning light, the tall pine looks commanding and stately, even though women, in their desperate need for firewood, had climbed the sixty-five-foot tree and hacked its branches off, leaving only a small, unbalanced crown of leaves, just enough to allow it to

breathe. As the sun lights up the surrounding ranges, the tree is obscured in the glare and seems to withdraw and merge into the hillside. And when the women come with their scythes in search of wood, they pass it by without giving a second look at its shorn and inconspicuous presence.

But at dawn, when the first rays of the sun touch the spur, once again the imposing pine comes into its own and draws attention with its sharp, clear lines etched against the dark hills.

*   *   *

The people from Danpur, in the higher ranges of Kumaon, have for generations woven mats from *ringal* grass—a type of bamboo that grows in dense clumps in the area. The intricate close-knit weave is from selected long rushes that can be woven without any knots, so that the strength and beauty of the mats is enchanced.

Even poor farmers invest in these, because they know that they will be able to use them for a lifetime. They have long-standing relationships with the Danpur farmers and welcome them into their homes when they come down from the mountains. The beautiful crafts they make with simple tools are much admired, and their dedication to maintain the purity of their tradition is inspiring.

*   *   *

The dense green foliage on the tree turned yellow and in a few days was ablaze with golden hues. But in a while the leaves began to flutter and dance in the late autumn breeze, and by early winter the tree was without its bright and colourful attire. It now stands bare and motionless, silhouetted against the mist.

The birds have gone, taking with them their song and lively chatter. And people come and cut away branches for fuelwood, leaving the tree truncated, without character and unnoticed all winter. But it stands anchored and unflinching for it must know that in spring the birds will nestle in its leaves, and people will enjoy its fruit and sit in the shade it provides.

*   *   *

The stray dog is beaten and shooed away from the village lane. It awaits its opportunity and darts into a door left ajar, grabbing the roti just cooked and dashes out, bearing its fangs at anyone who dares to come near.

But Dewan Joshi's son Hira is devoted to it, and plays with it as soon as he comes home from school. The little dog is transformed and follows him around like a gentle pup, roaming and scampering about the house and the fields.

*   *   *

The farmers came to know that one of the local officials had sold seeds to them at a higher rate than stipulated, keeping some of the benefit for himself. The farmers had now learnt from experience of similar happenings and could not be hoodwinked so easily. They felt it was high time that some action should be taken, so we got together and informed the district administration and an enquiry was instituted. As a result, the guilty official was transferred. He was so angered at our intervention that he got together a group of people to *gherao* me shouting slogans that an 'outsider' like me should not be allowed to stay for causing dissent and trouble in the village.

The people in the village came out protesting that the so-called 'outsider' was part of the community and even sent a petition to the state administration informing them about the harassment. Local officials realized that they could not ride roughshod over any of us, for we had built a strong bond within our community.

*　*　*

There is electricity in most of the village, but it is whimsical, and there could be hours, and sometimes even days, without any electricity. But people know that they can rely on the sun for light and warmth. As it moves up on the horizon, it sends early morning rays to Tara Dutt's house and then to Vijay Joshi's and Puran Negi's; from one ridge to the next, one house after another catches its warmth.

Everybody knows just when to expect it and each home opens its doors as it arrives. They know that it comes late in winter, early in spring and is wayward during the monsoon, but they know that it will come.

*　*　*

No amount of persuasion could make the women learn to read or write. They said that all their lives they had learnt only to take care of their families and their cattle, cut grass and collect firewood, and that was all they needed to survive.

But the new saving scheme required their signatures, as thumb impressions, normally used as an alternative, were not acceptable. The children decided that their mothers must learn to sign their names. With much hilarity and some heartbreak, they learnt to hold pens,

but their fingers refused to move as directed. The children badgered them to practice every day on scraps of paper and on kitchen walls with bits of coal, until slowly letters were formed and words took shape. And they could scarcely contain their joy on seeing their names on paper.

*   *   *

The white-cheeked bulbul with its jaunty crest, perched on the oak tree, preens itself, burrowing its beak into its feathers, and turns its neck to take in the surroundings. In a while its mate appears and they chirrup happily while continuing their grooming.

Smartened up for the day, they detach themselves from the rest of the flock engaged in noisy conversation and readying for the morning flight. They take off together unnoticed, and begin to forage around for berries and concealed insects in the brown patch where the snow has melted. They twitter and chirrup joyfully like children preoccupied with play and not really interested in food. One flits away mischievously and the other flashes past, intent in pursuit. They chase each other hither and thither, now on the snow-laden branches, now on the roof, and even close to where I sit. There is no concern about anything but their involvement with each other.

We are separated and lost amidst the jostling, milling

crowds, and events around us. And then his eyes find mine and we become oblivious of the throng.

* * *

The house that was there a minute ago is no longer visible, as the rising mist has submerged it. It is as if the artist, dissatisfied, has put a brush of white paint over the picturesque scene of hamlets and terraced fields flanked by high ranges receding into the distance.

He works ceaselessly for a few days, washing his canvas with rain and erasing with mist, until, at last, the striking scene emerges, with brown stubble fields under a canopy of vivid blue, tinged with the silvery light of fresh snow on the mountains.

The houses with sloping slate roofs reappear and the people within come to life, bustling with activity. And the delighted voices of the children ring out in the sunshine.

My little house hedged in on all sides was so complete a world for me. But the shadow mist veiling my life lifted, and I began pulling down my fences. I discovered the beauty of my surroundings and the remarkable people living there.

* * *

Nand Bahadur has few possessions, and even necessities like a kettle for tea, a bucket for a bath, and often the oil for the small lamp, are borrowed from neighbours. On days when Nand Bahadur does not find employment, he borrows money for the day's rations for the family. His wife, Mamta Devi, though pregnant, supplements their income by helping farmers in the fields with weeding, hoeing and carrying heavy baskets of manure for the crops. Indra, their daughter, who is six years old, manages her younger brother, but sometimes they fight and scream and disturb the whole neighbourhood. Mamta returns exhausted from the fields, meets their clamouring demands for attention and cooks the evening meal.

Mamta says that at this age they can deal with hardships, and the children do grow up somehow. But it is important that while she and Nand Bahadur have the capacity to earn they should minimize expenditure, to save for a secure old age.

I do understand their point but it is sad to think that they can have little interest in anything beyond the security of their small, closed world.

*   *   *

There are a host of birds in the area and if one has the patience to wait for them in silence, one is well rewarded with the presence of the black-throated jay, yellow-cheeked tit, spotted babbler, the Himalayan tree pie and others, too.

And now that the peaches and pear trees are bare of fruit, and there is no fear of being shooed away, the birds make their home in the thinning foliage. Their chirruping and singing starts at daybreak and goes on until they are preened and presentable to fly off for the day. As the evening light begins to wane, they return home and resume their prattle until they settle down for the night.

One morning, the farmer decided to prune his trees. The birds came swooping down that evening and flitted around, protesting noisily. Then they scouted around and flew to the pine trees further down, from where they continued their evening conversation. They accepted the ways of man in their carefree way.

* * *

The priest read out the *Satya Narayan Katha*. The discourse spoke of tales of princes who became paupers

and ordinary men who lost their kith and kin—all because Satya Narayan was displeased. A murmur went through the people as they recalled their own sorrows.

The priest continued to chant that devout men, inspired by gods, had written that a puja offered to Satya Narayan, followed by a feast, would fulfil the hopes of all those who took part. Bishan, who had stretched his resources to perform the puja, could feel the truth of the words. He felt sure that his son Kailash would be blessed and have a good life, and also that his fields would yield a good crop.

I may not know the source of my faith, but I am convinced that an ordered universe cannot run by itself. And I endeavour to seek the unknown.

*   *   *

Devaki Devi's daughter Bhagvati comes for the first time to my little library. She is all wrapped up in her mother's shawl and follows shyly behind her elder sister, Renu. She stands quietly with eyes cast down, unresponsive to all my efforts to make conversation with her, while Renu prattles away as she looks at the small collection of children's books.

Bhagvati moves forward hesitatingly and when I am not looking, picks up a book and gives it to her sister. As I record her name she steals a glance with her gentle eyes framed in a tiny muffled face, but looks away when I try to approach her.

But when she runs down to her house, other children gather around and she chatters away excitedly about her book.

*   *   *

Last winter, when the peach trees shed their leaves, this lone tree was wilted and dried. It seemed that it could not possibly recover and would have to go for fuelwood.

But the farmer waited and by early spring, tiny green shoots appeared on its bare gnarled branches. And in a few months, with the monsoon rains, its branches were covered with thick foliage and laden with fruit.

There are spells when I am out of tune with everything around me. But given time, the phase passes and I regain my composure.

*   *   *

Overburdened Mamta Devi relies increasingly on six-year-old Indra to take care of Pappu, the three-year-old, and Laxmi, the newborn. Indra sits by the fire and sings and talks to them the way her mother does, enjoying the role. But, after a while, the make-believe mother is exasperated. Placing the sleeping Laxmi gently on the floor in a corner of the room, she and

Pappu fight and play with abandon, scattering grains of rice all over the place, and chasing each other outside in the mist.

When I was made the chief guest at a function, I felt important and grand. But soon the charm wore off and I wanted to sit and chat as usual with the women from my village.

*   *   *

The trees stand bare and exposed and the green has gone from the countryside. Sheep have come down from the *bugyals*—the high grazing grounds. Flocks of birds, flying in groups, head southwards to warmer climes. There are a few butterflies fluttering around the yellow flowers on the drying pumpkin creeper.

Many farmers are leaving too, to visit holy shrines and relatives in distant villages, as there is little work to be done in the fields.

The claims of the city did not allow me to travel when it got uncomfortably hot or cold. But there was for me the bracing winter with its array of garden flowers; the onset of spring with tree-lined avenues coming alive with fresh new leaves; the hot summer with its bounties of melons and mangoes, and clear starry nights; and the cooling monsoon showers with the aroma of wet earth and freshly washed trees and shrubs.

*   *   *

Mamta is weeping outside her small room. The clamouring of her children does not distract her, for Nand Bahadur, who has just come back from Nepal, has brought the news that her father has died. She was married when she was seventeen years old and in the eight years since, she had not seen her father. The children, Indra, Pappu and little Laxmi, arrived one after another, so she could not take the long bus journey to Nepal and thereafter a six-hour trek home. The visit was put off each year to wait until the children were older and also when there was sufficient money for gifts for the family. Moreover, she had thought there was time enough, for after all her father, though old, seemed healthy.

She was consoled by the thought that he was well attended in his illness, and was taken to the big hospital and given medicines. But she repeated sadly to herself, 'Time does not wait for anyone.'

* * *

Shankar Negi took the cows to graze every day after school, along with other boys in the village. They spent hours chasing each other wildly in complete liberty, without any adult restraint. Sometimes they would make tea for which they would slyly milk the cows and sit around to talk of happenings in the villages, and of their hopes and dreams.

But there was a restlessness about Shankar and he would occasionally break away from the group to linger in the forest. He would spend hours looking across the valley to the barely visible houses of Bageswar town and beyond to the distant horizon.

One day Shankar was not to be found and someone said they had seen him at the bus station. His distraught mother, Krishna Devi, could do nothing but wait anxiously for news. She hoped that some acquaintance would see him by chance and prayed that he would write. But Puran, his father, began to think of his own thwarted dreams and remained silent.

In my younger days, I wanted to reach for the rainbow, but today, I am uneasy when my children want to wing their way afar, to unknown places.

* * *

The path leading to Bishan Kathayat's house was narrow and at some places large stones blocking the steep path had to be negotiated carefully. Bishan was concerned about the bridal party, which would have to carry the doli to bring Kailash's bride home after the forthcoming wedding. The people in the village rallied together to remove the boulders and to dig and shape the path.

The children of the family brought hot tea at regular intervals, which provided a welcome break for the men to jest about memorable episodes in other weddings in the village for which, too, they had worked together.

* * *

Last year, only three students in the village passed the board exams for the final school-leaving year. This year, the parents were very concerned about their children, for this exam would determine their future—the possibility of work in a factory or office, or even to get them to college for a career of their dreams.

During the exam period, Girdhar's mother, Krishna Devi, fell ill, so his father, Puran Negi, met him on his return from the examination hall at the bus stand. He told him that he was going to meet Abid Siddiqui—known to everybody as Nanne Mian—whose family had successfully cured illnesses in the village with herbs and roots. He asked Girdhar to go to Dewan Joshi's house, as he needed help to carry some wooden planks that were required for fixing his roof, and also to request him to lend a quilt for Krishna, who had shivered through the morning with a raging fever.

By the time Puran came home, Girdhar had just returned after taking the cattle to graze, but he now had to get down to helping his father with the evening meal. At the end of the day he was tired and went to sleep, and he went for the exam the next day without even having looked at his books.

And Girdhar was not an exception—Prem's father, Kundan Kathayat, had at long last got a job in the tea plantation, and his mother, Rekha Devi, could not manage on her own. Prem had to find time to take on some of the work: a pit had to be dug for storing the yams, as otherwise they would rot; the upland rice was to be scatter-sown, for which the fields had to be ploughed. And in between, he had to take the midday meal to his father at his workplace.

Renu was no better off. In the morning, on her way to the exams, she had to deliver milk to the regular customers in the small bazaar. And her mother, Devaki Devi, who was not well, sent her on small errands to the bazaar or to her neighbours who sometimes needed help in their fields.

The parents were happy that their children helped them with necessary chores. There was no time to talk to them about their examinations and no question of giving them any help or guidance. Somehow the future would take care of itself.

※   ※   ※

Radha and Renu had just finished their high school exams, and during the waiting period for their results, they decided to join a sewing class. The class was held in the market outside the village, where they happened to meet two young men who were recently posted to the local electricity department. On their way back from class, they would meet—'by chance'—the young men who were off duty and they would all walk back together on the road leading to their home.

One day, Girdhar and some others from the village saw the young men talking to Radha and Renu. They dragged the young men away and chastized them for daring to talk to girls from the village. The two girls ran home quite frightened and distressed.

Later, Girdhar spoke to Panuli Devi and Devaki Devi to warn them about the behaviour of their daughters. The reaction of the two mothers was most unexpected. They began to scold and abuse Girdhar for daring to question the morality of their daughters and also for tarnishing their reputation by spreading tales in the market. In fact they said that the only reason they did not take up the matter with his parents was because it would drag their daughters' names further into the painful episode.

The parents tried to support the changing attitudes of their children, but reluctantly and without conviction, which made them react sharply to advice that was close to their own thinking.

*   *   *

With the first light of day, Krishna Devi sharpened her scythe on a stone and went to cut grass for Pyari. Later, she rushed off to the fields, carrying the thickly woven mat on which she beat the harvested paddy to remove the grain. Just before leaving, she called out to her younger son, Girdhar, to bring her tea as soon as he returned from school.

But Girdhar started playing cricket with his friends and later got involved in watching a match on TV. Krishna was worn and fatigued from working all day in the fields and kept looking up towards the house for her son. She staggered home late in the evening to see him sitting cosily in the room and shouted at him.

He retorted insolently that despite being at school all day, he had delivered the milk to the market and watered the seedlings in the small plot, and so had earned his rest. This was the last straw for Krishna. She lost all self-control and hurled a string of abuses and accusations at him. She spurned his offer to help bring in the wood and to light the fire for the evening meal. With great effort and clanging utensils around, she started cooking and continued to berate him.

To drown her unceasing stream of words, Girdhar started the evening prayer and blew the conch and rang the bell louder than usual. Later, in a calmer mood, Krishna tried to approach him affectionately, but he remained aloof and hurt the whole evening.

*   *   *

It has been an unusually dry and stormy winter. The snow on the mountains has receded to the very top ridge, exposing dark granite slopes. There is disquiet and concern that this will have an adverse effect on the streams that emanate from these mountains and feed the mighty rivers flowing to the plains. Thoughts of failed crops and famine flash in my mind.

But with last night's snowstorm, the mountains glisten in their pure white raiment trailing right down to the ranges within reach. And I am reassured that the rivers will flow after all.

I get so worked up about things beyond my control.
But there is so much within my reach, where I could
make a difference.

*   *   *

The lights gleaming in the valley below are slowly
going out. It is the magic hour of dawn, but plummeting
temperatures have kept people indoors. The spotted
babbler and the crested black tit have not emerged to
chirrup and dance on the dry branches of the pear and
peach trees, which stand undisturbed like phantom
guards.

There is an air of expectation, and silently,
unannounced, the snowflakes come floating down
gently. Now they come faster, appearing like a white
sheet fluttering mysteriously without a breeze. The
pine trees quickly don chic white coats and the dry
branches of fruit trees glisten with pearl droplets. And
even as we look, the whole panorama is transformed
with a spotless white cape draped across the mountains
and valleys, accentuating the stillness.

*   *   *

For two years, Bishan Kathayat and Gopal Dutt had
stopped all contact between their families. The problem
started over some forgotten trivial event, which got
aggravated because Gopal's son used abusive language
and even threatened Bishan. Gopal's children stopped

using the short cut near Bishan's house and took the longer route to school.

But now Bishan's only son, Kailash, was getting married, and this was, for him, the last great duty to be performed. And somehow it stirred feelings of goodwill within him, even towards Gopal, for, after all, he had known him since childhood. He realized that if he let this opportunity slip, the rift would be irreparable. From Gopal's side, too, there was a thawing, as one of his sons had had a bad accident and though Bishan had not come himself, Kailash had visited him in the hospital.

Emissaries deployed by both sides handled the situation diplomatically so that both Bishan and Gopal retained their pride and self-respect. Gopal was persuaded to respond to Bishan's request to send his wife to help clean the rice and pound the spices for the feast along with other women in the village. This opened the way for Gopal to be invited to the wedding. Both men went into the prayer room where tilak was applied on Gopal's forehead. After that there was no question of hard feelings, and the evening was spent reminiscing about the time when their sons were born.

The bitterness of their quarrel, in a way, reflected the strong bond that existed between them. Others could not rebuild the bridge for them; only the two friends could know the old markers lost in the wilderness of anger and hurt.

* * *

We got up earlier than usual to catch the morning bus, only to see it drive past just as we reached the road-head. All our hollering and shouting was lost in the rattling of its old frame.

We then had to wait for two hours until the next bus came, and could do nothing but walk around disconsolately to keep ourselves warm. As we turned the corner, the first rays of the sun glistened from behind the ridge. And even as we watched, the glow spread on the horizon unveiling a whole range of peaks stretching as far as the eye could see, from Panchchuli in the east to Chaukhamba in the west.

The mist drifted away revealing a group of women in colourful saris walking towards terraced fields freshly washed with the morning dew, children running about tending cattle grazing in the stubble-fields and two old men in earnest conversation near a small shrine at the edge of the field.

The honking of the bus broke the bewitching silence, reminding us that two hours had slipped away.

Last evening I stepped out on a whim to find a bejewelled sky, and a gentle breeze caressed my face . . . and the hours sped in the silence. My impelling drive to make gainful use of my time had found a more meaningful expression.

It has snowed non-stop for three days and now the sun is struggling to find a way through the dense clouds. We step out into a veritable fairyland with houses, trees and mountain ranges adorned in gleaming white. Our footprints are etched sharply in the fresh snow.

Sunlight begins to stream through the tall pine trees and a shower of snowflakes cascade to the ground. The black-throated jay and the yellow-cheeked bulbul twitter and flutter, momentarily revealing their presence. Nothing else stirs. Our breath, accompanied by a ring of vapour, is strangely loud.

I was marooned by the heavy snowfall. But as the days of waiting extended in these quiet surroundings, the silence drew me into its peace.

*   *   *

Over the past few months, people had been facing great difficulty in collecting firewood for the long cold winter, as they were no longer permitted by the government to cut trees in the neighbouring forest. They were dependent on wood fires to cook and to keep themselves warm and now in winter, firewood was fast running out.

Their misery was heightened by the snowstorm which lashed their homes and the surrounding forest. But in a while when the trees heavily laden with snow came crashing down, it seemed that the gods had answered their prayers. Unmindful of the snow, they fanned into the forest to claim the fallen trees. The sound of the axe was silenced only in the dark, when people returned home delighted with their unexpected load of wood.

I thought with concern of all the possible eventualities. But events unfolded at their own pace and opened avenues undreamed of.

*   *   *

The surrounding haze had blanked out all visibility for days and there was no hint of life. But today, curling smoke from the rooftops is discernible. Shadowy figures sitting around glowing embers begin to stir and soon voices can be heard.

The women are calling out to each other, for the fodder supply has run low, and picking up their scythes they hurriedly head for the forest. The men start walking towards the market hoping to find some labour and the older women bustle about immersed in neglected household chores. The children revel in the snow for no school is possible.

The unpredictable weather and the disruption is part of the reality and is taken in their stride. They get back to work as soon as they can and once again life takes on its rhythm. Unlike them, I am flustered when there is a disturbance in my regular routine and it takes time to fall back into step.

*   *   *

Puran Negi's father died about twenty years ago. Puran often talks about him and every year on his death anniversary, the *shradh* ceremony is done in the house with great solemnity. Puran does not take on any jobs for two days, even though it means loss of wages, as the preparations start on the day before the death anniversary. On the first day Puran fasts, so that when he meets the priest on the following day, he is pure and in the right frame of mind. The prayer is centred on his father but also includes all male ancestors up to two generations. A similar ceremony for his mother's death anniversary includes the female ancestors.

Puran's son Girdhar, who is now studying in Almora, has come up especially for the occasion, and relatives from the neighbourhood are also invited for the prayer. The priest, whose family has been presiding over religious functions in Puran's family for several generations, conducts the prayers feelingly, for he was a good friend of Puran's father.

The solemnity ends with a note of happy remembrance, with special food prepared in memory of the departed souls. The priest is the first to eat, and leaves with his traditional gift of clothes and a stipulated payment. The children then get down to enjoying the food with gusto. They were not even born when their grandfather died.

Puran tells Krishna, who feels the expense is too much, 'What use is my income if I cannot even venerate my parents? After all, they brought me into this world and taught me to stand on my feet.'

The ritual for my parents is limited to a bunch of flowers to mark occasions that were especially important to us. But their memory is evoked often, when a shared moment comes to mind.

* * *

Devaki's elder daughter, Renu, was almost seventeen years old, and now that she had finished high school, her mother was anxious to get her married. Devaki was constantly living with the fact that she was a widow and had to manage alone, and there was Bhagwati, the younger daughter, also to be considered. Someone known to the family suggested an eligible young man of the same caste. He was an only son whose family was comparatively well off, as both father and son had jobs in Delhi. True, they lived in a remote, isolated hamlet, but at least Renu would go to a comfortable home.

Renu had had only a glimpse of Sham Dutt, her prospective husband, and could not really form any opinion about him. In any case, the marriage was a foregone conclusion, for what could she say when her mother looked so relieved to have found someone suitable for her?

The excitement of the wedding, new clothes, the

mandatory mangal-sutra and the adventure of a new life engaged Renu. It took her a few days to adjust to her surroundings, but Sham was kind, and made her happy when he said that he would take her to Delhi with him.

When it was time for Sham to return to work, Bhaguli Devi, his mother, firmly refused to allow Renu to go with him. She said that Renu could follow sometime later as she was required to work in the fields, which could not be managed by her alone. Sham agreed without any protest, and without saying anything further to Renu about it, went off to Delhi.

The house was divided between Sham's father and an uncle with whom the relationship was not good. The uncle would drink heavily every evening and abuse his brother's family, especially when Sham and his father were not around. It was a nightmare for Renu, who had never experienced such language and behaviour in her simple home.

As days went by, it became obvious to Renu that her mother-in-law was the one who ruled the family and that her chances of going to Delhi to live with her husband were remote. Her mother-in-law was determined to get Renu to do as much work as possible in the fields and in the house, so that, at long last, she could now have her rest. Renu had no neighbours near enough to whom she could go for a little respite, except the young daughter-in-law next door.

Soon enough, Renu realized that she was pregnant, but there was no let-up in the work. Her mother-in-law ignored her complaints of fatigue and pain and said that when the time came, the midwife from the nearest village would be there for her. There was no question of Sham coming home for the event. However, the midwife could not handle the complications and the baby died, leaving Renu completely shattered and weak with the experience. Bhaguli was unfazed and said that that was Renu's karma and even a doctor could not have helped her; in fact, it would have been a waste of money to call him.

It was clear to Renu that Sham could not do anything for her, as everything depended on Bhaguli. And her own mother had started thinking about the marriage of her sister. The only person who could help her was she, herself, and the thought awakened her resolve.

*   *   *

Hansram's brother Narayan Ram had never really done well in life, and when his wife died after their sixth child, he was a broken man. His eldest child, Ganga, was only twelve years old and all the rest were younger and needed attention and care. Narayan, who just about managed to provide for the family, was helpless in the face of this calamity. Ganga, who was in the fifth standard, had to leave school to cook for

the family, look after the newborn and do what she could for the rest of the children.

In three years time, when Ganga was fifteen, Narayan was relieved that he could find a match for her. Though the young man had not finished high school, at least the family was better off than his own. Ganga, being a gentle, good-natured girl, did all her mother-in-law's bidding, so things went well for a while.

But after a few years, when Ganga did not show any signs of having a child, the in-laws began to nag and taunt her. Her husband, though kind, could not really stand up for her, and her father was too weighed down with his own problems. Somehow she found the strength within herself to brave the verbal onslaughts. But one evening, when she had to be isolated because of her monthly period, the in-laws spoke more harshly than ever of the barren woman in their midst, while her husband sat there mutely.

She sat on the doorstep and wept as she had never done before, and then went quietly into the cattle-shed, where, like other women, she had to sleep in her 'unclean' state. She waited until all was still and then went to the small shed where the dry grass was stored and, pulling a rope across the rafter, hung herself.

* * *

Most of the able-bodied men in the village have gone to the plains for jobs, as their small landholdings do not yield enough even to feed their families. The hard-pressed women are left to manage field and family on their own, and have devised a system to get manual labour for their numerous tasks.

Sunita Devi has several oak trees, so she barters the leaves—which are valuable fodder—for help in hoeing and weeding the paddy fields. Panuli Devi has a tract of uncultivated land with plenty of grass, and Mamta Devi, who needs the grass to feed her cow, helps Panuli to carry manure down to the fields. Krishna Devi's cow has just calved, so she gives a glass of milk every day to Mohan Ram for tea for his family and he pays it off by ploughing her fields. Mohini Devi, whose house is on the uplands, has sufficient *mandua*, the coarse millet grain in demand for food in winter, which she barters for help in chopping firewood.

There is also the *alta-palta*—the mutual exchange of labour in each others' fields—which brings the women together to talk and sing as they work, relieving the drudgery of working long hours alone.

Even in the most difficult circumstances, we find a way because of our natural tenacity for survival.

*   *   *

The flawless white snow melted, leaving a few white patches, which in a few days turned into messy, muddy pools of water encircled by sludge and silt. This morning, the bitter cold froze the water into luminous sheets of ice. As dawn broke, the pink hue blended with the blue of the sky and the green tones of the pines in a beautiful kaleidoscope of colour on the ice, glistening in the midst of swampy ground.

* * *

Every day at dawn, I sit on my balcony and see the morning sun sending its magic light to wake the towering peaks shrouded in shadows. One by one, starting with Trishul, which makes a spectacular appearance right in front of me and, going from east to west, from Panchchuli to Chaukhamba, taking in Nanda Kot, Nanda Khat, Nanda Devi, Nandagunthi and Gori Parbat, the whole range awakens, beaming radiantly. I could not ask for a more beautiful start to the day.

As I sit there soaking in the beauty, my thoughts turn, too, to the end of the long days' journey. The people in their disarmingly honest way bring home to me that I am one of the oldest people in the village. And reassure me warmly, 'You have passed three score and ten, which is a good age, but don't worry, and stay with us. We will take you on your last journey on our shoulders'.

They accepted the law of nature as a matter of course. But I still have to come to terms with it as naturally as they do.

* * *

As soon as she got up, even before making tea, Krishna Devi opened the door to the cowshed and let out the bullocks and Pyari with her calf. The cow went obediently to the yard to be tethered to her particular post, but the calf started suckling and had to be dragged away. Krishna ran up to the haystack and brought out a few sheaves that she distributed amongst the animals. She then sharpened her scythe on the stone platform and walked briskly towards the oak trees to cut the leafy branches. She worked her way up and stopped short of the top to ensure that her tree could breathe and survive, and came back with a staggering load of leaves.

Krishna selected young green leaves for Pyari and her calf, while putting a pile of leaves in front of the bullocks. She started to milk the cow, coaxing her and talking to her gently, but there was just a trickle in the pail, so she untied the calf that came bounding toward its mother to suckle. After a few minutes, Krishna dragged the calf away and got down to milking again. With much coaxing and scolding she managed to collect less than half a pail and, muttering half to herself, she said, 'Pyari, after all I do for you, is this all I get?'

My friend responded to my generosity within the limits of her capacity. But still, I felt let down, because I had not understood her limits.

*   *   *

It was a winter evening and already dark. A young boy who had come on an errand from a neighbouring village could not get back in time to catch the bus home. He stopped hesitatingly at Puran Negi's door, who, on hearing his predicament, invited him to share the evening meal. Then Puran quietly asked Krishna Devi to sleep with the children and without much ado shared his bed with the stranger.

Before leaving, the boy bent low in front of Puran and Krishna in respectful farewell, and they in turn gave their blessings. It was no matter that they would probably never see the boy again, as their time together had been well spent.

*   *   *

Narayan Ram had never worn any kind of footwear. Even when going to a wedding dressed in his best clothes, he was always barefoot. People looked at him with sympathy, murmuring that he was too poor to buy himself a pair of shoes. After all, he was a labourer and had a large household to support.

But one day when someone ventured to ask him why he could not purchase even a pair of simple slippers, Narayan replied, 'We take off our shoes outside a temple in reverence to God. And I want to keep this veneration with me all the time.'

*   *   *

Vijay Joshi's uncle Shiv was eighty-five years old and much respected in the family, who gave him affection and all the comfort they could provide. But at his age, he yearned for a life of quiet, away from the constant prattle and noise of a bustling household. So the small unused cattle-shed at the end of the field was cleared up for him and he lived there peacefully.

He cooked his own simple meals and always saved a few scraps for the two stray dogs in the village. In a corner, he deliberately dropped a tiny lump of sugar from which a line of ants moved to and fro, engrossed in their activity. On the ceiling of the room he fixed bits of cloth to serve as tiny hammocks, and birds flitted in for shelter when it rained or snowed. His quiet companions brought him the peace he sought.

He did not say much, but

everyone who visited him took something of his serenity with them.

* * *

The alpine pastures in the upper reaches of the mountains, known as bugyals, are still under snow. The shepherds have been down for a few months in their village, ploughing the land, repairing their homes and cattle-sheds. This is also a time to be with their families, to enjoy festivals and weddings.

But now they are restive and wait impatiently for the snow to melt, for then the bugyals will welcome them with a fresh green carpet tinged with the pastel colours of spring blossoms. Their flocks of sheep will thrive and fatten on succulent grass and acquire splendid woollen coats. And the shepherds will again find the freedom of the mountains.

I am captivated with the antics of my grandchildren in the city. But after a while my thoughts drift to the small cottage in the secluded hamlet where I live, in contact with the inspiring Himalayas.

* * *

Shankar seemed to be glad to be back after his mysterious disappearance about which he spoke little, and his bedraggled look was enough to evoke the sympathy of his parents. Now he was very helpful about the house and every morning he took the cow and bullocks to graze.

One morning there was a loud cry from Shankar that one of the bullocks had fallen in the rocky ravine near the stream. Krishna and her younger son, Girdhar, ran out of the house, and Girdhar dashed across the field, jumping over terraces, past the stream to the small gorge where the bullock lay in a heap.

Krishna began to moan softly and, overcome with grief, fell to the ground without uttering another sound. Her husband had bought the bullocks with borrowed money so that they would no longer be dependent on neighbours' bullocks for ploughing their fields and would be able to sow their rice on time. The thought of the near impossibility of returning the loan froze her mind.

Hearing her sons shouting below, Krishna pulled herself up with great effort and walked towards them. She found that a crowd had already gathered there, talking excitedly and giving advice. Someone suggested that the bullock could have consumed a toxic plant and so lost its balance. Another brought a large lemon from the tree near his house and forced it down the animal's throat, as it was an acknowledged cure. The old man next door, known for his experience, approached the bullock with a prickly branch of the kilmora bush and passed it over its body while reciting a mantra. He shook the branch repeatedly in a procedure known as *jhardna*, shaking off the evil spirit, and pronounced that the animal would be all right.

Encouraged by this, three or four of the younger men lifted the bullock and made it stand. Though it was unsteady, it was clear that there were only a few bruises but no broken bones. The stomach was bloated and the animal was badly shaken and moved very slowly, pulled and pushed by the men. Meanwhile, Krishna, surrounded by women, kept repeating over and over again that she had some kind of premonition of ill-luck and had told Shankar not to take the bullocks out, but he had insisted on it. One of the women spoke of her own sad experience when a snake had bitten her cow, which never revived in spite of the injection given to it by the doctor.

Another said that her bullock had become listless after eating a poisonous grass, but the man who had done the jhardna had some goodness in him, for her bullock recovered. Krishna listened to them all, but was not comforted as she walked slowly with the group, inching their way up to the house.

The bullock was tethered in the gote and given powdered coriander. Slowly the crowd dispersed, and Krishna sat outside waiting for Puran. Word had already got to him in the bazaar, where he had gone to deliver a head-load of vegetables for a farmer. He was troubled when he saw his wife sitting forlornly and comforted her saying, 'We cannot lose heart. We have led honest straight lives and God will surely spare our bullock.'

Krishna was too distraught to even eat dinner. Puran appeared calm but neither of them slept that night. In fact, he went outside frequently, and by the morning, he had smoked a bundle of bidis, which normally lasted a week. Before taking his load of wood to the market, both sat in silent prayer before the deity, and then Puran performed a jhardna with eagle feathers and told his wife confidently that the bullock would now recover.

However, both Shankar and Girdhar felt that a doctor should be consulted and went to Gurur, an hour's bus ride away. On hearing the symptoms, the doctor prescribed an antidote for the poison grass. The two boys felt reassured that with this medication the bullock would get better.

By the next day the swelling in the stomach had greatly reduced, and the bullock started eating the fresh green oak leaves given to it. Some said it was the jhardna that helped the bullock to recover, while others were convinced that it was due to the medicine.

*   *   *

A thick mist looking like a billowy lake encircled by dark blue mountains submerged the valley. Slowly, an unrecognizable green and yellow object emerged from the mist. The older people were disquieted by the strange phenomena and, despite explanations about the effect of light, took it as an ill omen.

As the shadowy dawn receded, it became evident

that the early rays of the sun penetrating the haze had glowed surrealistically on the spur projecting into the valley. The illusion slowly vanished as the sun rose in the sky and the spur emerged with its pine trees and yellowing bushes. But still some held on to the belief of an other-worldly vision.

We all interpret things within the limits of our own understanding. And no matter how it appears to others, we can only go by our own logic.

*   *   *

Kamla Devi had to struggle to bring up her children after her husband Kesar Dutt's death. All she had was the produce from the small fields and the irregular wage income that her young son brought home. Although her husband's brother Gopal lived near by and was comparatively well off, he did not help, and, in fact, had even tried to take away her land. As a result there was little contact between the two families. Gopal did not even attend his brother's funeral.

But when Gopal died, Kamla Devi's family went into a twelve-day mourning as is customary. Even her son, who was studying in another village, was informed that he had to observe all the rituals and cook his food without turmeric, onions and garlic. For what needed to be done, had to be done.

However, despite all she did in the face of grave

injustice, Gopal's family reprimanded Kamla because her son did not take time off from his studies to be present for the mourning period.

*   *   *

Over the years, the mild and gentle Panuli Devi had become very autocratic. She had total control of the household and dominated her daughter-in-law. She took charge of the small children while the young woman had to run around at her bidding, doing all the chores at home and in the fields. Panuli would brook no interference or even suggestions; everything had to be her way, be it the purchase of clothes and sweets for festivals or any small thing needed for the house. She decided which crops had to be sown in each field and doled out the seeds herself. No decisions were left to anyone else.

When Panuli Devi fell ill, her four daughters came home to look after her. Even from her sick bed, she ordered them about as they scuttled around giving her medicines and food. Someone was always there to press and massage her aching body, but she became weaker and weaker and it came to a point when she could barely speak. One morning, as her daughter-in-law, who had taken charge of the household, was taking out the lentils for the afternoon meal, Panuli cried out that that was not to be touched, for it was kept for next year's seed ... And those were her last words before she died.

*   *   *

There was a commotion in the village because a sack of potatoes brought for the wedding of Mohan Ram's son was missing. It happened on a rainy night when everyone was indoors and nobody from another village could have walked on the slushy path. It had to be someone from the community. There was much conjecture in the village and the suspicion fell on poor old Narayan Ram, who had taken to drinking to forget the tragic death of his daughter Ganga. He was always short of money, and only two days earlier he did not even have enough to buy daily rations for the family.

The real story came out when Leela Devi's daughter spilled the beans. Apparently two of her companions had removed the sack from the gote to make a little money. She had been a silent partner but felt free to talk, as she did not get her share of the booty. The parents of the two boys were enraged when they heard that their sons had been involved in the theft and distraught at the thought of the disgrace it would bring to them. But the two mothers were even more concerned about protecting the boys and begged their husbands to pay Mohan the cost of the potatoes so that the matter would go no further.

*   *   *

Pyari was to calf again and there was nervous expectation in the household, for if all went well the cow would give milk which would be sold in the market, assuring the family of an income for several months. Everyone was up early, for Pyari was restless and they could tell that her time was near. And even as they watched, she gave a tremendous heave; but instead of the calf, part of her intestines came hanging out. There was confusion, dismay and fear, for they had never experienced this kind of a situation.

Fortunately, Shankar, Krishna's elder son, was at home and he hurried to Chanauda, the village five miles away on the main road, to fetch the veterinary doctor. The doctor readjusted the offending intestines and soon established that the calf was positioned wrong. He got hold of the calf's hind legs and tied them with a rope, and with Shankar's help, he pulled firmly but gently till the calf slid out. He said that Shankar should accompany him to bring some necessary medicine.

When Shankar returned, the medicine was poured into a hollow bamboo and his brother Girdhar forcibly opened Pyari's mouth, while his father, Puran, administered the medicine. Pyari seemed calmer as they sat and stroked her, calling her gently by her name. But until she began to eat grass and drink water, there was concern and anxiety. And for several days, one member of the family was always there, giving Pyari jaggery and lentils to bring back her strength. It was a great relief when she recovered even though it was upsetting to hear from the doctor that the condition of the calf was not good, and that its chances of survival were slim. This also meant that the cow would now give little or no milk.

Shankar had been taking care of the calf from the time it was born and had become very fond of her. He used to feed her himself and carry her out into the sun. He was disconsolate and distraught to see her so ill. He crept out at night to be with the dying calf. He bent over it and lifted her head on his lap, and stroked her gently in the silence.

*   *   *

The salesman came down the path, his frame leaning to one side with the heavy weight slung on his shoulder. As he called out, 'Bangles for sale, bangles for sale', Sunita Devi came out of the house eagerly, for she had been wanting to replace the broken glass bangles on her embarrassingly bare arms.

She balked at the price and told him, 'These two remaining bangles on my hands are brighter and thicker and I paid less for them.' He replied, 'This is the first sale in the morning—the *bonee*—which sets the tone for the rest of the day, so I cannot reduce the price. But, if you like, you could give me old cans and broken implements in part payment.'

Her son Hira and his cousin Sunder scoured the untidy dump behind the house and came back with a rusty heap, which the salesman arranged in small piles and announced with a professional air that it all weighed nine kilograms. The young men protested and asked him to weigh it for them. But as he could not carry around the heavy weighing measures and the family did not have any scales, they had to take his word for it. He offered a pittance of one rupee per kilogram for all the battered hardware, pointing out that the transport to the recycling factory in Haldwani would reduce his earning to a bare minimum. The family could not counter his strong argument and had no option but to get rid of the junk. Moreover, the barter enabled Sunita to get away by paying a few rupees less for the bangles. The salesman picked up a sizeable rock and proceeded to flatten out all the cans and stuffed them into a large sack, which he swung on his back. And heaving his wares on his shoulder, he set off on the path, calling out, 'Bangles for sale, bangles for sale.'

Sunita looked at her bangles and felt happy to think that she had got a bargain and the salesman felt sure that this good bonee would bring him more luck.

* * *

The mountains have cast aside their winter veil and gleam in the clear sunlight. Days of clear blue skies have convinced the farmer that at last the severe winter is over. There is a flutter of activity as ploughs are brought out, cleaned and repaired. And reluctant, resistant bullocks that have been grazing and resting for months are dragged out and yoked to the plough. With loud cries and urgings, the farmers coax the bullocks to move forward in the fields, while women and children break the clods of earth with wooden mallets to loosen the soil for the ploughing.

But winter is not so easily dislodged and summons cold winds from the north. The trees, which stood proud and erect along the bare fields, sway uncontrollably, and clouds appear from seemingly nowhere, carrying rain and sleet. The dismayed farmers with half-ploughed fields unyoke the bullocks and take them home.

But, though disappointed, they know that winter is fighting a losing battle, and that spring is definitely on the way.

*   *   *

The young boy walks to the distant hill with his cows, and watches over them all morning as they graze contentedly. He sits under the oak tree, motionless for a long time. Absently, he pulls out his flute and plays the purest notes, expressing the captivating melody of his surroundings.

We need to discover for ourselves the instrument that expresses the music with which we were born. Or else we lose that which gives us our own special melody.

*   *   *

And now today . . .

I can no longer run up the hill and climb the *kaphal* tree, and I have to keep stopping to catch my breath. I prefer to rest awhile under the shade of the chestnut tree with my companions of old, and munch delicious, fresh cucumbers with spicy chutney. We talk of our respective childhood days, and of all that has happened in all the years that I have spent with them: of the old people who are no longer there; of the new brides and children in each family; of the hardship of people whose sons have had to leave the village to find jobs; of Golu Maharaj, Narsingh, Bhairavnath and other deities who guide their lives . . . and, as we sit there, the radiant light of the mountains reaches us, magically unchanged.

In the village, where everyone shares their joys and sorrows, it is easier to accept the natural flow of life and death, which even children understand in their own way, for these events are played out again and again. The firm base in their lives, which holds them together in good times and bad, is the conviction that an honest life will bring them salvation and that even if they stray, there is always a second chance, the opportunity to get back into the fold.

The mountains here are believed to be the sacred abode of the gods—Dev Bhoomi—and religion is a part of daily life. Every evening in every household, the tinkling of bells can be heard mingled with the sounds of the conch shells and chanting, as they perform the *arti*.

The serenity here has made me aware that there is a path—though not visible—that I want to explore. In the process, I have discovered that in one way or another, in our own manner, we are all linked in this quest. And the distinctions and divisions I had made in life were in my own mind, for idylls are idylls anywhere. And whether we live in the mountains or by the ocean, in cities or in villages, in the East or in the West, the wisdom and experience of all ages is there for everyone, if we but search for it.